ICFA Continuing Education

Managing Investment Firms: People and Culture

Proceedings of the AIMR seminar *Managing the Investment Professional*

April 2, 1996
Chicago, Illinois

Gary P. Brinson, CFA
David I. Fisher
J. Parker Hall III, CFA
Luke D. Knecht, CFA
Richard S. Lannamann, CFA, *Moderator*
Thomas M. Luddy, CFA
David A. Minella
Patrick O'Donnell
Stuart M. Robbins
Claude N. Rosenberg, Jr.
James F. Rothenberg, CFA
Alison A. Winter, CFA

Edited by Jan R. Squires, CFA

ICFA Continuing Education is published monthly eight times a year in January, April, May, June, Augus September, October, and November by the Association for Investment Management and Research, P.O. Box 3668 Charlottesville, Virginia 22903, U.S.A. This publication is designed to provide accurate and authoritativ information with regard to the subject matter covered. It is sold with the understanding that the publisher is nc engaged in rendering legal, accounting, or other professional services. If legal advice or other expert assistance i required, the services of a competent professional should be sought. Periodicals postage paid at the post office i Richmond, Virginia, and additional mailing offices.

Copies are mailed as a benefit of membership to CFA® charterholders. Subscriptions also are available a US$100 for one year. Address all circulation communications to ICFA Continuing Education, P.O. Box 3668 Charlottesville, Virginia 22903, U.S.A.; Phone 804-980-3668; Fax 804-980-9775. For change of address, sen mailing label and new address six weeks in advance.

Postmaster: Send address changes to the Association for Investment Management and Research, P.O. Box 366 Charlottesville, Virginia 22903.

ISBN-13: 1-879087-65-0 ISBN-13: 978-1-879087-65-1
Printed in the United States of America
August 1996

Contents

ICFA Board of Trustees, 1996–97

AIMR Education Committee, 1996–97

AIMR Senior Education Staff

Foreword

The investment management business has undergone rapid changes in recent years. Investing no longer stops at a country's borders; ticker tapes have been replaced by computer screens; and phys-icists are now being hired by Wall Street firms to model these increasingly complex markets. But one vital aspect of this business has not changed; invest-ment management is a people business. The success of a firm depends on how successfully it manages its people resources, and as all the participants in this proceedings attest, managing investment pro-fessionals begins with managing the investment firm—creating the structure and processes that define how the firm will operate.

There are probably as many approaches to managing an investment firm as there are firms because every firm is unique, which must be reflected in the firm's culture and structure. The authors in this proceedings represent a wide variety of successful approaches, and although each author's approach is slightly different, they all share some common beliefs: Firmly establishing and clearly communicating a firm's culture, or philosophy, is crucial; managing begins in the hiring phase; and creating a rewarding, challenging, and fun environment is essential for motivating highly intelligent individuals with diverse backgrounds. All of the authors in this proceedings have met the challenge of managing their firms in the face of constantly changing technologies and resources; they have recognized that the key to success is managing the professionals who work for them.

We wish to thank Richard S. Lannamann, CFA, Russell Reynolds Associates for serving both as the moderator of the seminar and as a presenter. We also extend our appreciation for their valuable contributions to Gary P. Brinson, CFA, Brinson Partners; David I. Fisher, The Capital Group Companies; J. Parker Hall III, CFA, Lincoln Capital Management Company; Luke D. Knecht, CFA, Russell Reynolds Associates; Thomas M. Luddy, CFA, J.P. Morgan Investment Management; David A. Minella, LGT Asset Management; Patrick O'Donnell, Putnam Investments; Stuart M. Robbins, Donaldson, Lufkin & Jenrette; Claude N. Rosenberg, Jr., RCM Capital Management; James F. Rothenberg, CFA, Capital Research and Management Company; and Alison A. Winter, CFA, Northern Trust Bank of California, N.A.

We hope you find the comments of these highly respected investment professionals useful in managing your own firm or your own career.

Katrina F. Sherrerd, CFA
Senior Vice President
Educational Products

Biographies of Speakers

Gary P. Brinson, CFA, is the founder, president, and managing partner of Brinson Partners. Previously, he served as president and chief operating officer of a major investment management company. He is a former executive committee member and past chair of the Institute of Chartered Financial Analysts. Mr. Brinson is currently a member of the Editorial Advisory Board of *The Journal of Portfolio Management*, a trustee of the Research Foundation of the Institute of Chartered Financial Analysts, and a trustee of TIAA–CREF. He holds a B.A. from Seattle University and an M.B.A. from Washington State University.

David I. Fisher, chairman of the board of The Capital Group Companies, is a portfolio manager for global, non-U.S., and emerging market assets with responsibility for Capital's international investing activities. Prior to joining Capital, Mr. Fisher was a second vice president and financial analyst for Smith Barney and a marketing executive with General Electric Company. He is a founding member of the International Society of Security Analysts and a trustee of the Lowe Institute, Alternative Living for the Aging, Claremont McKenna College, and Harvard-Westlake School. Mr. Fisher holds a bachelor's degree from the University of California at Berkeley and an M.B.A. from the University of Missouri Graduate School of Business Administration.

J. Parker Hall III, CFA, is president and managing director of Lincoln Capital Management Company. He is a former president of the Investment Analysts Society of Chicago and currently serves on the boards and the investment committees of the University of Chicago and the Chicago Symphony Orchestra. Mr. Hall is the author of several articles published in the *Financial Analysts Journal*. He holds an undergraduate degree from Swarthmore College and an M.B.A. from Harvard University.

Luke D. Knecht, CFA, is an executive director with Russell Reynolds Associates in the Investment Management Practice. Prior to joining Russell Reynolds Associates, he served as president and chief investment officer at CSI Asset Management and at Harris Investment Management. Mr. Knecht is a director of the Investment Analysts Society of Chicago. He holds a B.A. from the University of Colorado.

Richard S. Lannamann, CFA, is managing director and global head of Russell Reynolds Associates' Investment Management Practice and is cohead of the firm's financial services sector. Previously, Mr. Lannamann served as senior vice president and portfolio manager with Management Asset Corporation and as a vice president in the research division of Smith Barney. He holds an A.B. in economics from Yale College and an M.B.A. from Harvard Business School.

Thomas M. Luddy, CFA, is managing director and chief investment officer of J.P. Morgan Investment Management and is also a member of the firm's Global Management Committee. In previous positions, he managed U.S. equity portfolios and was responsible for the Equity and Balanced Accounts Group in the United States and for global equity research activities. Mr. Luddy holds an undergraduate degree from St. Peter's College and an M.B.A from The Wharton School of the University of Pennsylvania.

David A. Minella, president of LGT Asset Management Inc., is responsible for all retail and institutional asset management activities. He serves as director and executive committee member of the Liechtenstein Global Trust and as president and chair of the GT Global Mutual Funds, which is an investment advisor to the GT Global Funds. Prior to joining LGT, Mr. Minella was employed by Putnam Investments as corporate treasurer, president of Putnam's Trust Company, and vice president of marketing and sales. He is a member of the board of governors of the Investment Company Institute and a trustee of Bentley College. Mr. Minella holds a B.A. in accounting and finance from Bentley College.

Patrick O'Donnell is managing director and chief of global equity research for Putnam Investments. Prior to joining Putnam, he served as president of Exeter Research, as both managing director of international equities research and a member of the board of directors at Prudential Securities, and as a vice president/analyst at Furman Selz; Donaldson Lufkin & Jenrette; and E.F. Hutton. Mr. O'Donnell holds a B.A. from Harvard College and a Ph.D. in English literature from Princeton University.

Stuart M. Robbins is managing director of institutional equities at Donaldson, Lufkin & Jenrette. Prior to joining DLJ, he served as vice president and retail industry specialist with PaineWebber and as vice president, research department comanager, and retail industry specialist with C.S. McKee. Mr. Robbins is a member of the AIMR Nominating Committee and a past president of the Merchandising Analysts of New York. He holds an A.B. in history from West Virginia University and has studied at the graduate level in law at New York University and in business at the University of Pittsburgh.

Claude N. Rosenberg, Jr., is a founder and principal of RCM Capital Management. Previously, he was employed at J. Barth & Company. In addition to numerous articles on finance, Mr. Rosenberg is the author of four books on the stock market and investment management. He has lectured extensively on the field of investments and is past president of the Stanford Business School Alumni Association and former chair of the Stanford Business School Advisory Council. He holds a B.A. and an M.B.A. from Stanford University.

James F. Rothenberg, CFA, is president and director of Capital Research and Management Company. He also serves as vice chair and director of Capital Guardian Trust Company; president and principal executive officer of The Growth Fund of America; president, principal executive officer, and trustee of American Variable Insurance Series; director of The Capital Group, Capital Group Research, and Capital Guardian Trust Company, a Nevada Corporation; and portfolio counselor for Capital Research and Management Company. Mr. Rothenberg is a director of Huntington Memorial Hospital and a trustee for the Westridge School for Girls. He holds a B.A. in English from Harvard College and an M.B.A. from the Harvard University Graduate School of Business Administration.

Alison A. Winter, CFA, is president and chief executive officer of Northern Trust Bank of California, N.A. She is former director and president of the Investment Analysts Society of Chicago, former director of the Financial Analysts Federation, former governor of the Los Angeles Society of Financial Analysts, and former chair of the Asset Management Committee of the American Bankers Association Trust Division. She holds a B.A. from San Francisco College for Women and an M.B.A. from the University of Chicago Graduate School of Business.

Managing Investment Firms: An Overview

Jan R. Squires, CFA
Professor of Finance
Southwest Missouri State University

Investment professionals face significant challenges from the "technical" side of the business—a plethora of asset classes, exotic instruments, ever more sophisticated investment strategies, and always, the breakneck pace of changing technologies and developing markets. But what about the "people" side of the business? In the rightful focus on managing money and serving clients, how much time is, or indeed can be, spent thinking about the management and leadership issues that permeate investment management firms? Might the challenges facing the people side of the business be as important as, or more than, those on the technical side?

Even cursory thought given to the management of investment professionals reveals the complexity of these people challenges. How does the firm recruit, motivate, retain, and reward the infinitely varied, immensely talented, and highly creative people who are attracted to this business? How does the firm create careers that capture their imagination and give them satisfaction and, at the same time, harness their energy and drive to serve the welfare of clients? Do common management principles exist—basic leadership fundamentals that cut across organizational size and type, investment style, and geographical boundaries?

This proceedings is the product of an AIMR seminar intended to give participants the time and opportunity to ponder these many and tough management questions by taking their cues from some of the most respected and successful firms and managers in our industry. The authors consider a variety of issues, challenges, and opportunities in managing investment professionals and organize their thoughts into three broad areas.

- Management philosophy and culture. How important is a firm's culture in setting the tone for effective management? What are the elements of a workable management philosophy? What should be the role of the "star versus team" debate in shaping a firm's philosophy and culture?
- Management fundamentals. Do immutable management fundamentals exist? How should the firm go about the "nuts and bolts" of people management—recruiting, training and developing, evaluating, and compensating? What are the true motivators in this business, the real determinants of job satisfaction?
- Special management situations. Does globalization entail additional management challenges? What are the unique issues encountered in managing sell-side professionals or in leading those investment professionals who deal with individual clients?

Management Philosophy and Culture

A key—perhaps the key—management task at the highest level of the organization is forging a coherent philosophy that guides and a culture that pervades: a philosophy and culture that are consistent with organizational objectives and that can be owned throughout the organization.

In describing Brinson Partners' organizational culture, Gary Brinson defines an investment organization's culture as a group of people who have a common set of beliefs; knowing and understanding that culture, which may differ markedly from the culture of other firms, is vital if people individually, and the firm collectively, are to thrive. Brinson uses three "word equations" to characterize his firm's organizational culture. In turn, this culture is operationalized and the guiding principles are executed through a set of nine core beliefs—ranging from total teamwork, to uncompromising integrity, to a performance meritocracy—which are applied throughout the organization. These core beliefs are accompanied by several ancillary observations that further affirm Brinson Partners' philosophy and culture.

David Fisher discusses several elements of effective organizational culture. Particularly important, he argues, is creating an environment that builds on the strengths and interests of talented people and that recognizes the benefits imparted by cultural and personal diversity. He casts a critical eye on oft-repeated management "truths" with regard to centralization and counters with his own formula for assessing the trade-offs involved in the decision to centralize or decentralize. Fisher closes by setting forth seven elements of management success, including the dangers of overmanaging and the importance of having fun; for Fisher, managing investment professionals is not unlike managing any other group of highly talented individuals. In fact, he concludes by relating how a discussion with a soccer coach made him realize the universality of many management tasks.

James Rothenberg provides an interesting conclusion to the discussion of management philosophy and culture by arguing that the age-old star versus team debate misses the point of management effectiveness. Management, he contends, is custom built to reflect the firm's goals and desired ambiance. For Capital Research and Management, that custom-building process centers on a relentless recognition that the investment business is a people business, results in a portfolio structure that uses multiple managers, and relies on a measurement and reward system that channels competition against competitors and markets rather than internally. Rothenberg closes with a critical look at the strengths and drawbacks of star and team approaches; he concludes that the choice for any firm must be consistent with its goals, culture, and resources.

Management Fundamentals

Certain fundamental tasks of management seem to be immutable; investment organizations—whether large or small, value or growth oriented, domestic or global—must attend well to at least a few "basics."

J. Parker Hall argues that a clearly defined and tenaciously held investment philosophy provides a bridge between organizational culture/management philosophy and management fundamentals. Why? Because a firm's investment philosophy—in the case of Hall's firm Lincoln Capital Management, large-capitalization growth stocks—drives other management activities, particularly the investment process, the measurement of performance, and the compensation of employees. Hall outlines Lincoln's very traditional field-based investment process, which relies on time-tested P/E valuation disciplines but which also incorporates what many would see as nontraditional investment decision-making approaches. He points out how several important management tasks—recruiting, benchmarking, and compensating, for example—fit within the context of Lincoln's investment philosophy and process.

Claude Rosenberg continues the discussion of management fundamentals with his claim that attention to certain basic, perhaps even simple, tenets may raise the level of leadership in an investment organization. Hiring the right people is a critical management task, and judging how people will react to "down times" is an especially vital part of the hiring process. A related, equally important element is the manager's stance in the face of poor judgments and missteps, namely, the ability to help people learn from their inevitable mistakes. Modeling productive work habits and creating effective working disciplines are also important; Rosenberg provides several examples of both. He concludes with a call to encourage and reward creativity and innovation; systems designed to do so can include both monetary and nonmonetary elements.

Drawing on the context of managing a relatively large research department, Patrick O'Donnell focuses on three key tasks—recruiting, developing and challenging, and evaluating and compensating. In-depth assessment of candidate traits, including some traits not typically examined by most firms, and an exhaustive interviewing process are characteristic of Putnam Investments' recruiting and hiring process. The difficulties in developing and challenging investment professionals are legion; O'Donnell addresses such issues as designing career-long development opportunities, confronting the trade-off between conformity and creativity, dealing with mistakes, and creating ownership within the organization. He concludes by raising a variety of issues that are embedded in the process of evaluating and compensating investment professionals and by describing Putnam's approach to compensating analysts.

Motivating people is an obvious and staple management activity; Luke Knecht and Richard Lannamann contend that examining employee job satisfaction provides a window into motivation factors. They present the results from a survey of AIMR members designed to examine levels of job satisfaction in the investment industry from several perspectives. More than 80 percent of the respondents indicate job satisfaction, with satisfaction levels being highest among general managers and portfolio managers and among professionals working in mutual fund companies, investment counseling firms, plan sponsors, and endowments/foundations. The most important positive job satisfaction factors, or motivators, are largely "internal" in nature—professional achievement, for example. In contrast, the most important negative factors—for instance, company policy or administration—are more "external" in nature. Knecht and Lannamann highlight differences in job satisfaction levels and motivating factors by type of organization, functional area, size of organization, and tenure with organization and age.

Special Management Situations

As important and universal as are guiding philosophy and management fundamentals, specia management situations do arise that call for new insights and approaches.

Creating a global investment organization, for instance, challenges even the most resource-rich firm. Thomas Luddy provides an overview of J.P. Morgan Investment Management's approach to building a global investment network. JPMIM uses a three-step approach that emphasizes the role of research analysts in creating, capturing, and communicating an information advantage. Two particularly important management issues in that approach center on creating a rewarding environment and choosing a predominantly local versus predominately global perspective. Luddy also details several other success factors in the JPMIM approach, including the ability to leverage size and specialization, the role of teamwork and collegiality, and the importance of effective communication.

Also addressing the globalization theme, David Minella draws a distinction between domestic dominant and virtual global investment firms. The specific management challenges for a virtual global organization, argues Minella, are creating a common vision and goal, implementing strategy, making decisions, operating efficiently, and compensating appropriately. Solutions for these challenges arise out of a system of timely bottom-up communications, an organizational structure that clearly links accountability and responsibility to development and compensation, and a management approach that distinguishes between decisions that affect clients and decisions that affect the firm. Minella concludes that all such solutions must cut across geography, language, and culture.

In a counterpoint to oft-stated industry opinion, Stuart Robbins presents a compelling case for the important, indeed increasing, role of the sell-side professional in our "information overloaded" industry. High-quality distribution of usable information is vital in enabling the resources of a money manager to have a positive impact on a client's portfolio, and managing the people who provide that information can be a challenging task indeed. Robbins, however, contends that managing sell-side professionals comes down to seven relatively simple "truths," ranging from recruiting well and giving full account responsibility, to highlighting corporate culture, to refusing to manage by fear. Most management problems, he concludes, are caused when managers simply choose to abdicate their management role. Says Robbins: "If you are going to be a manager, manage."

Although many principles of effective management are fairly constant and ultimate investment objectives are more or less universal, Alison Winter argues that a number of issues pose special challenges in managing the investment professionals who deal with individual clients. After detailing several factors that distinguish individual- or private-client accounts from institutional accounts, she sets forth seven components for success in managing individual-account managers, including effective leadership, appropriate incentives, and necessary technology. Investment firms have different organizational structures and different ways of addressing management activities and functions; highlighting these differences or choosing a particular structure, Winter concludes, is less important than recognizing and reflecting the characteristics and needs common to managers dealing with individual accounts.

Conclusion

Whether discussing management philosophy, fundamentals, or special situations, the authors in this proceedings share one common trait: They "pull no punches" in bringing their unique experiences and opinions to the table and in holding up their own firms and careers for scrutiny to provide answers to the difficult "people" questions that investment firm managers face daily. The result is a thoughtful and balanced look at managing in the investment industry—a look that ranges from conceptualizing culture and philosophy at the highest levels of the firm to actualizing processes and decisions at the lowest, a look that fully recognizes and indeed celebrates the diverse talents and needs of investment professionals, a look that never questions that people are the most important resource in a business that ultimately rises or falls on the quality of its service to clients.

Organizational Culture

Gary P. Brinson, CFA
President and Managing Partner
Brinson Partners, Inc.

Because organizational culture varies among investment management firms, knowing and understanding the firm's culture is important for people to be able to yield maximum results for the organization and for themselves. Specific "equations," beliefs, and observations serve as the guiding principles for the organizational culture at Brinson Partners.

The concept of organizational culture may appear at first glance to be narrowly focused; upon reflection, however, it is actually an amorphous concept and one that is quite difficult to define. In some ways, I liken it to religion. The world is filled with different religions, and one is not necessarily better than another. Different people join different religious groups because they have a common set of beliefs. An investment organization is much the same—a group of people who have a common set of beliefs (i.e., the organization's culture); one particular set of beliefs (organizational culture) is not necessarily better than another, and the rich variety of organizational cultures is one factor that keeps the investment management profession and industry vibrant and interesting.

Precisely because organizational culture varies among investment management firms, knowing and understanding the firm's culture is important for the people who belong and thrive in that culture to yield the maximum results, not only for the organization but also for themselves. This presentation addresses Brinson Partners' organizational culture, first, by looking at the "equations" and beliefs that serve as our guiding principles and, second, by highlighting some ancillary observations that have evolved from those principles and that help us operate effectively.

Guiding Principles: The Equations

Any culture needs principles that people can understand. We describe Brinson Partners' organizational culture with three word equations:

Philosophy + People + Process = Performance (1)

Performance = Investment results + Client service (2)

Maximum performance = Maximum business results (3)

The first equation shows that performance—the cornerstone of our business—is a function of the philosophy the firm adopts, the people in the firm, and the processes the firm follows. The second equation indicates that performance is made up of investment results and client service. The third equation illustrates that maximizing performance maximizes business results. This framework is not special or unusual, but it is a simple, straightforward one for everybody to focus on and understand.

Guiding Principles: The Beliefs

In our business, describing our principles is relatively easy; executing them, however, is not. By putting these words (equations) into operation, by executing the principles, the fabric of the organizational culture is woven. Because we have worked with these equations for many years, we do have some experience, as well as some scars and bruises, from creating a culture that people can adapt to and that creates the right type of fabric for the organization.

Specifically, the way that Brinson Partners has put the equations into operation and executed the guiding principles can best be explained through the core beliefs applied in our organization.

- *Teamwork is the collegial interaction and collaborative activity that form a common bond for achievement.* An organization may want to focus its efforts in this way for many reasons. For example, I have no experience working within a star system

I have always been part of an organization in which professionals collaborated and worked together. Our firm does not have a "star"; if we were to go to the star system, we would fail because none of us is of that caliber. None of us is singularly smart enough to carry the load for our clients; therefore, almost out of necessity, we need to collaborate and work together to achieve the objectives that we all want to achieve. Other firms could just as correctly say that they do not have to use a team approach because they have bright people who can stand on their own. I am not sure that one method is better than the other; the choice depends on the circumstances. All I can do is define what works for us.

This team approach may be easier to implement in our firm than in some others because we do not have separate profit centers. We have one firm and one profit center. We do not pay people on the basis of assets under management; we pay them for value added relative to benchmarks. Once a firm moves away from profit centers and ceases to use assets under management to determine someone's pay or rewards, operating as a team becomes much easier.

Interviewing people for teamwork skills is, however, difficult. When a firm is talking about bringing people into the organization, whether they are young and just out of school or older and more experienced, determining whether they agree with this philosophy—not merely as a set of words but as the actual actions of the individuals—and if they will be happy in this type of firm is very important.

- *Execution supersedes intention.* Almost everyone is well intentioned. Intentions, however, do not count for much. Our firm has a cultural mind-set that tries to dissuade people from thinking about such things as "I intended to do this" or "I wanted to do that." Execution is what matters. Get the job done no matter what that job is, whether it is picking up a piece of paper on the floor or making a trading decision. Get the job done; move beyond merely talking about intentions.

- *Quality in everything we do preempts quantity.* We do not necessarily want to be a larger organization in terms of assets under management or size of staff; we do want to be very good at what we do. We have no ambitions to be the fastest growing firm or the biggest firm, but we do have an ambition to be the best firm. We try to get people to think about devoting resources not to being bigger but to being better. We try to get people to do less but to do what they do exceptionally well. This mentality is hard for a firm that grows and changes over time, but it can be contagious. A firm can have people stimulate and cross-train others to focus on the trade-off between quality and quantity in their daily activities so that they understand that what matters is the quality of what is done, not the quantity.

- *The pursuit of excellence must be pervasive and unrelenting.* Investment management is one of those businesses in which last week's, last month's, or last year's success is not worth anything in terms of whether or not the business will be successful next week, next month, or next year. Knowing this fact allows us at Brinson Partners to understand that we cannot become overly confident; we cannot be complacent about what we have achieved. No immutable law or principle says that because an investment management firm has been successful, it will continue to be successful.

This situation is different from, for example, manufacturing. If a company is manufacturing a product and has mastered the process—the product comes off of the assembly line with the desired quality and integrity—the company's management can say that the process worked yesterday and will probably work tomorrow because we have the manufacturing of this product down right. Investment management does not work that way; the pursuit of excellence must be ongoing. People can take pride in what they have achieved, and we want them to, but to lose sight of this pursuit of excellence is a big danger.

- *There are no higher ethical values than truth, honesty, and professionalism.* We try hard not to manage by fear or force, but when it comes to this statement, we do use fear and force. We literally scare people on this one subject. We take a very strong-handed approach when it comes to ethics. We constantly remind people in writing and verbally of the standards of conduct that we insist upon in an ethical, honest, and professional organization. We use a lot of material from AIMR's *Standards of Practice Handbook*, and we make sure our people read it. Beyond that, all we can do is let people know that we will not tolerate any breach of ethics and that we will take extraordinary actions should any violation ever occur.

In the 20 years that I have been in the business, we have had no violations that would fall into this category of integrity breaches. My biggest fear, however, is that I will wake up tomorrow and find that someone within our organization of 375 people has violated the standards of conduct, ethics, and professionalism of our business, which are very fragile. All we have collectively is our integrity. If the firm is tainted or damaged by anyone, that person violates the entire organization.

- *Commitment, dedication, and hard work are our instruments of success.* Occasionally, one finds people in any walk of life who think they are so naturally talented or gifted that they do not have to work as hard as the people next to them—that they can get by with less commitment and dedication because they are "better" people. In our firm, we prefer that those "better" people work somewhere else. They would not fit well within our culture. We like people who are committed to what they are doing with dedication, hard work, and long hours, and we talk about that commitment as a firm and reinforce that set of beliefs within the organization.

Enjoying ourselves and maintaining a pleasant working environment are important elements of success. People have to be in an environment where they get professional satisfaction and, hopefully, enjoy what they do. As an organization, we need to supply the resources and environmental characteristics so that people enjoy coming to work and performing the tasks in their areas of expertise. We probably invest back into our organization as much as, and maybe more than, some other firms in terms of creating a satisfying environment for our people, allowing them to enjoy their workplace, and doing as much as possible to heighten their professionalism and accomplishments.

Individual rewards are tied to a performance meritocracy. People must understand that the merit of what is done is what matters. Whether a person has 25 years of experience or his or her brother-in-law is a celebrity does not matter. What matters is the merit of an individual's accomplishments. Fortunately, this approach is widely considered in the industry as the correct way to manage and create a culture and is not unique to Brinson Partners. Nonetheless, continually reinforcing this belief in people's minds, particularly as individual responsibilities change over time, is important.

We will always benefit from critical review and a goal of constant improvement. At Brinson Partners, professionally critiquing peers and superiors is not only permitted but encouraged, although we expect criticism to be done in a way that does not attack the individual. We try hard to encourage self-evaluation, criticism, and the ability to deal personally with that criticism. The biggest mistake we make in investment management is working hard to research an idea, concept, or strategy; putting the idea into place in the portfolio only to find a week or a month later that all that work, time, and effort was done wrong; and not admitting the error. Individuals who think highly of themselves find it difficult to admit that the strategy they put in place or the stock they bought was a mistake. Admitting mistakes is the hardest thing to do, so people tend to find reasons why they did not make a mistake.

We probably cannot encourage or reward people enough for the courage to say they were wrong; bad investment performance can come from decisions if we hang onto them or play them out too long in the wrong direction. Creating a spirit in which people understand that it is acceptable to be critical and to ask critical questions at a professional level is important. Managing critical employees is not always easy, and some people are not as tactful as they should be. I am sure some people do not want to work in our organization because of this one cultural belief. Criticism is healthy and necessary, however, and it is a cultural item with which people have to be comfortable.

Ancillary Observations

Over the years of trying to execute our guiding principles and to operate by our core beliefs, we have developed some ancillary observations that further elaborate our organizational culture and help us to operate effectively.

- "Success comes to those who increase their worth. To increase your worth, you have to do more than gain new knowledge and skills. You have to become the kind of person with whom others like to work." We try over time to inculcate this belief into our people, particularly the younger people joining our organization. We try hard to point out that having knowledge and skill and improving on that knowledge and skill are not enough; to be successful within our organization, an individual has to learn how to work with others. Other people have to look upon the individual as the type of person with whom they can associate, communicate, and interact, rather than as "standoffish"—a talented person doing a great job but not very approachable. When that situation has arisen at our firm, we have found that, no matter how talented or skilled that person might be, other people tend to gravitate away, leaving that person isolated. A major part of a person's worth to us as an organization lies in her or his ability to be considered by others to be a collegial person to work with—someone who is willing to be part of the process and part of the organization—and a person who contributes on a fair basis.
- "The greatest ability is dependability." This statement says it all concerning many of the daily tasks that must occur in an organization. Whom can we depend on to get the job done; who are the "turn to" people?

- "Enthusiasm makes ordinary people extraordinary." Given a choice between a highly talented but introverted, self-serving, and unenthusiastic person and another person who is not as smart but very enthusiastic, I will choose the enthusiastic person every time. The enthusiastic people may not have the highest test scores or may not have gone to prestigious colleges or universities, but they will fit much better within the culture of our firm. They will be more productive and happier in the firm and in the contributions that they can make to our success.

Conclusion

Words are often inadequate to capture important concepts; nonetheless, as an organization, we have embraced these "words"—equations, beliefs, and observations—to define our culture, to behave in a fashion that produces that culture, and most importantly, to make sure that the people in our organization understand the culture and its composition. Our stance reflects our belief that organizational culture provides the intangible element within which people can best work together for our clients' welfare and for the current and future success of our organization.

Question and Answer Session

Gary P. Brinson, CFA

Question: How do you keep a culture fresh and alive and not allow it to become outdated?

Brinson: We try to take an active role in creating the corporate culture. When we get together each year at our annual meeting, we spend one hour discussing our beliefs and the culture of the firm. We solicit ideas about who we are and how we should think about ourselves. Ultimately, some of these beliefs, such as truth, honesty, and professionalism, will not change. Other aspects, however, can and should change over time as our organization grows and changes. We have no formal process for cultural change, and I cannot give you a good answer as to some managerial way that we deal with change. It is a natural evolution.

Question: Do you use any external feedback mechanisms from customers or vendors to measure how your culture is perceived or is evolving?

Brinson: About every 18 months, we send a survey to our clients about the level of service, integrity, and so forth, either as it applies to the firm or to the person on the account. Unfortunately, this approach is a fairly ill-structured form of feedback. It would be useful to get feedback in a systematic fashion over time, and we perhaps should hire some outside expert to do so for us.

Question: Is a change of ownership a threat to corporate culture?

Brinson: Yes. We are blessed right now by the fact that we have acquired worldwide investment operations from Swiss Bank Corporation: The sky is sunny, the weather is nice, and we have a tailwind. What will happen when we hit that inevitable squall or storm and life is no longer perfect? Will outside people come in and say we need to change this or that? I have no ready answers to these questions. I do know that a firm's culture is extraordinarily sensitive to organizational change, and we must be careful to make sure that we can keep our culture in place in whatever form the organization takes.

Question: You appear to have a very generalized approach to culture. Is that preferable to a more precisely "engineered" approach?

Brinson: No. Anything that fits the organization can work. In my mind, the worst thing that could happen is not that a firm chooses the "wrong" approach to culture but that a firm does not know what its culture is. If you know what your culture is, you can be successful. Firms that are not successful, not simply investment firms but any organization, do not know their culture. As long as an organization knows its culture, taking one path or another does not matter.

Words of Wisdom on Managing a Global Investment Firm

David I. Fisher
Chairman of the Board
The Capital Group Companies, Inc.

Structuring an increasingly global organization and managing investment professionals in such an organization demand focus and energy. The most important principles, however, may be simple—remembering that investment management is a people business, being skeptical about so-called management "truths," and attending to a few basic tenets of organizational success.

For most of the first three decades of The Capital Group Companies' existence, our organization was what David Minella would classify as "domestic dominant" (conducting domestic work from a central location), but we have moved toward becoming a "virtual global" organization (a truly global organization with decentralized decision making).[1] Slightly more than 35 percent of Capital's $200 billion in assets under management are invested internationally or globally. Our client base is in more than two dozen countries. We have 3,400 employees worldwide, and of the 200-plus associates involved in the investment process, more than 20 percent are located outside the United States. International investing has been the fastest growing part of our business.

I have learned some things from an exposure to the evolutionary process that has brought Capital to the point reflected in these statistics. This presentation focuses on my personal observations drawn from 28 years of experience in the investment management business, including 26 years with Capital. These observations center on the people nature of the business, to centralize or not to centralize, the key elements of organizational success, and the wisdom imparted to me by a soccer coach. Although Capital might, in fact, disclaim much of this presentation, I have found these ideas helpful in influencing the direction of an increasingly global organization and in managing investment professionals.

[1]See Mr. Minella's presentation, pp. 46–48.

Never Forget: This Is a People Business

The most important lesson I have learned is never to forget that investment management is a people business. I firmly believe that any number of organizational approaches can work, but each approach is ultimately dependent on talented people. The key to success, therefore, is the attraction, motivation, and retention of talented people. Too often, managers argue about filling a position; we much prefer finding a talented individual and then designing a position around the abilities, interests, and aspirations of that individual.

In addition, cultural diversity is critical in a global investment management organization. Capital now employs analysts and portfolio managers who were born in 30 countries. Rather than looking for individuals to fit some well-articulated mold, organizations would be better served by seeking people who will add a new dimension to the talents that are already present in the organization. These individuals need to have values that are consistent with those of the organization, but beyond that caveat, to be different is to be better. Looking for highly qualified individuals who can add another dimension to the talents currently present in an organization is a lot more complicated than merely filling a position, but it pays off handsomely in the long term.

To Centralize or Not: Beware of Truths

The issues associated with managing a global

investment management organization tend to generate considerable passion. Some people contend that for a global investment organization to be successful, it must be thoroughly integrated and centrally controlled. Some believe passionately that all investment professionals must be in one location for communicating effectively and for leveraging individual insights. Other people stress that the successful organization must be geographically dispersed and should require only modest overall coordination; only in this way can the organization be sensitive to the local requirements of doing business. Some argue strongly that the people making investment decisions must be completely in touch with the individual markets (i.e., located there) and that being successful requires a multioffice approach.

As for making investment decisions, some people are absolutely certain that every manager must have the ability to make cross-border decisions. Others insist, with equal passion, that nobody can know everything about everything and, therefore, the answer is in establishing country experts who pick the stocks while someone "higher up" in the organization decides on the asset allocation among countries.

I favor none of these "truths." I believe in the following formula about the investment process:

Proximity × Distance = Perspective.

What this formula indicates is that every global organization, in order to be successful, must know what is going on locally (in terms of clients and markets), which can only be accomplished by proximity. At the same time—and certainly from an investment perspective—the organization must be able to distance itself from what is going on in that locality. Only by bringing these two aspects together (proximity and distance) can an organization gain perspective. For example, I have always been struck by the fact that big turns in local markets are seldom seen by people who are there; such turns are more often identified by people who are distanced. This observation applies to U.S. and non-U.S. markets.

Elements of Organizational Success

From being involved in the management of a global investment organization, I have formed several opinions about what works and what does not work in today's rapidly changing environment.

- *The most efficient answer to an organizational issue is often not the most effective.* When a conflict arises between efficiency and effectiveness, choose the latter. Consensus building is not a very efficient way to make business decisions, but it tends to be an effective means of getting a group of independent thinkers to work together toward a common goal.
- *Investment success is about anticipating change.* Developing a computer simulation that explains the past is not difficult, but figuring out how the future will differ from the past is very difficult. The investment business is about predicting the future, not the past.
- *Where companies are located will become decreasingly important in the future.* Investment firms need to organize in a way that is consistent with this trend toward de-emphasizing location. It is obvious to me that a Swedish specialist could not do as effective a job analyzing Astra or Asea as would, respectively, a global drug analyst and a global electrical equipment analyst.
- *Investment organizations have to act locally and think globally.* This phrase is more than a clever play on words. To compete in a country, organizations have to be able to deal with local regulations, practices, customs, and standards, but they also have to have a sense of how they fit into the world.
- *Be careful of profit centers within the organization.* Attempt to broaden the definition of success rather than narrow it. The greater the emphasis on profit centers, the more time wasted on issues associated with expense allocations and fee flows and the less time available to do things that benefit the client.
- *Do not overmanage the effort.* Service businesses, including the investment management business, lend themselves to flat organizational structures. Hierarchies tend to be counterproductive. Leadership is best accomplished by example rather than by telling others what to do. The advice that logically follows is that managers will be more effective if they are also individual contributors in some aspect of the business.
- *Having fun is important.* Fiduciary responsibility and laughter are not inconsistent. This business is so all-consuming that encouraging everyone to work at making the exercise fun for all those involved is important.

Conclusion: Wisdom from a Soccer Coach

I recently had the opportunity to talk with the women's soccer coach from Georgetown University. By education, he is a dentist, but by dedication he is the soccer coach of a relatively new Division program that competes against the best teams in the country. He talked about what it was like to build the program from scratch. He compared coaches of well-established programs to piano tuners who have high-quality components (players) and only have to perfect how the keys (individuals) play together. He, on the other hand, had to first build the "piano," and he looked forward to the time when he could focus on fine tuning. When asked what he was looking for in a player, he replied with "heart, dedication, spirit, individuality, and compatibility." He talked about the time and sacrifice it took to build a meaningful tradition and a winning program. Perhaps most importantly, he said, the players must want to attract others that have more talent than they do to the team.

Upon reflection, I was struck that the issue of managing investment professionals in a global organization is often made overcomplicated; it is made to sound like an incredibly unique and difficult assignment, but it need not be. Like the Georgetown coach, the leader needs to figure out whether he or she is building an organization from scratch or simply fine tuning. After that, the leader needs to recognize that the challenge is all about people—attracting highly talented and very competitive individuals and helping them define success in terms of the team as a whole as opposed to their own needs and aspirations. This process describes what managing a global investment management firm is all about: first, deciding on whether the task involves building or fine tuning and, then, attracting, motivating, and retaining talented individuals to get the job done. My hunch is that the Georgetown University women's soccer coach could handle such an assignment quite well.

Question and Answer Session

David I. Fisher

Question: Which is more important, proximity or distance?

Fisher: Neither is more important. Both proximity and distance are necessary to make effective investment decisions. I would hate to be in an organization in which the only factors that were considered concerned the local investment environment. I would also hate to be in an organization in which all investment decisions were made from a remote location. This business is about building people, making them a part of the team, and making them more capable investment professionals in the future. I would assert that people develop and improve by experiencing the tension between proximity and distance. People who spend their entire careers focused only on the Japanese markets, for example, would be missing the opportunity to work globally and to gain that perspective. Organizations need to work at helping their people appreciate the complexity of the investment business at both the local and global levels.

Question: Can you decentralize decision making without duplication?

Fisher: No, it comes back to the trade-off between efficiency and effectiveness that I discussed. If more than one person is making the same kinds of decisions, then by definition, efforts are being duplicated. Having one person is more efficient than having several people make those decisions, but I would argue that the client is better off having two, three, or four people involved in that process. At Capital, we are willing to settle for the inefficiencies associated with duplication of effort in return for the insights and benefits that we think we get; or, to put it another way, we value the overall effectiveness of what gets done over someone's perception of efficiency.

Question: How can teamwork be promoted?

Fisher: You cannot start with words; you have to start with basic values—how you lead your life and what kind of an example you set. You cannot devise a scheme that encourages one kind of behavior and then have others—leaders of the organization—act in a different fashion. Teamwork is about the way people behave. At Capital, one of the things we make clear is that we are very slow to judge people, especially negatively, except when it comes to integrity and internal competition. Behaving without integrity has no grace period. Also, beating external competitors is tough enough; we do not have the time and energy to worry about competing with each other. Everything in the organization has to be consistent with that philosophy of teamwork. Therefore, the important issue in encouraging teamwork is to live it and breathe it every day.

Question: What is the most important issue for managing a firm?

Fisher: People, particularly concerning the generational changes that are taking place. This business is not good at managing generational change, as shown by the fact that organizations tend to be most successful when they are young, or when the founders have the biggest impact, and not as successful when the firm matures and leadership changes. The focus for managing a global investment firm has to be people—giving responsibility early to younger people and retaining senior associates' sense of organizational pride and ability to communicate values, enthusiasm, and culture without the need to hold on to management responsibilities and titles.

Question: Do you use "locals" for analysts or U.S. analysts living overseas?

Fisher: We use both, but we clearly use a greater number of non-Americans in our non-U.S. offices. It is more a function of an individual's interests and aspirations than where he or she was born.

Question: With people from diverse cultures, how do you create and implement a common set of values and vision?

Fisher: It starts with the interviewing process. Before being hired, an individual meets lots of Capital people. We talk a great deal about values and vision, and I suspect a self-selection process is taking place. After an individual is hired, we work hard at making sure that he or she spends a great deal of time in different offices working with lots of associates, and we have a number of gatherings that encourage people to get to know each other in informal settings. Finally, we talk constantly about our values and what we want to accomplish in the years to come. I suspect that the most important dynamic is that you have to believe in the values enough that everyone is willing to work very hard to ensure that they are maintained.

Star versus Team Approaches: Missing the Point

James F. Rothenberg, CFA
President
Capital Research and Management Company

The star versus team debate may miss the point. The management structure of an investment firm is custom built to reflect established goals and desired organizational ambiance. Any management approach will have strengths and weaknesses and should be constantly changing; most would benefit from a focus on only a few key issues, such as people resources, portfolio structure, and reward systems.

When consulting firms characterize investment management organizations, they discuss results, style, investment philosophy, organizational depth and breadth, quality of people, and size. They rarely address the star versus team conundrum. Perhaps that is because the star versus team debate as an absolute proposition misses the point. Management in investment firms is custom built; it is designed around the goals the firm establishes and the organizational ambiance that the firm's managers desire.

For instance, we have tremendous difficulty at Capital Research and Management thinking about the investment management process and managing our investment professionals without starting with our own sense of mission. We are first and foremost an investment management business. Our driving motivation is to produce consistently superior long-term investment results for clients and shareholders. We want to create and offer products that are truly long term and have enduring value. We want to resist the temptation to maximize short-term cash flows. Our mantra is long-term investment results. These defining characteristics drive how we think about our organization and how we try to manage our investment people. This presentation addresses key issues—people resources, portfolio structure, and reward systems—in pursuing such a bottom-up approach to managing investment professionals, and it closes with a critical look at the star versus team debate.

Investment Business = People Business

David Fisher continuously reminds us that the investment management business is a people business.[1] People resources are critical; they dwarf technology or any other variable anyone might cite as being the key determinant of success.

The people in this business are bright, unique, highly motivated, and highly paid; they are often prima donnas, volatile, and egotistical. The more successful they have been in the past 12 months, the more these characteristics may be accentuated. So, we recognize and accept the multifaceted nature of the investment professional and the unique and challenging set of characteristics that successful people in this business bring to the table.

Another important observation is that these talented individuals are highly mobile. They all can find extraordinary opportunities to ply their trade elsewhere, and they often get ridiculous offers when another firm becomes desperate or determined to fix an investment problem or attempts to take a quantum leap up in its investment management capability. Keeping the talented investment professional happy and challenged is an important ingredient in the successful and productive investment firm. Inevitably, happy means well compensated, but it also means more than that. Happy relates to satisfaction, to recognition of achievement within the organization, and to the firm's atmosphere or culture.

[1]See Mr. Fisher's presentation, pp. 9–11.

Portfolio Structure: Multiple Managers

All of the people resources culminate for the client in the portfolio management process. A critical aspect of this business relates to how organizations select portfolio managers; after selection, the most important issue is how the process itself is structured and how the professionals are rewarded.

One of my long-time colleagues, Jim Fullerton, has emphasized three fairly simple questions to ask when selecting a portfolio manager:

- What is the manager's record? What are the long-term (the longer term the better) results?
- What are the factors that contributed to those results?
- How likely are those factors to continue into the future?

The last point is critical. It is asking: What is the validity of an investment record as a logical predictor of future results? The regulators will not let us promise a future return, but that is what the prospective client or shareholder wants—not necessarily a promise of a certain percentage or dollar return but a belief that we will do as well in the future as we have in the past versus our competitors and the markets. The shareholder wants to be assured that what we have done in the past is predictable and that we will be able to deliver comparable returns in the future. Fullerton's questions are invaluable in forcing us to remember those client wishes as we structure our portfolio manager process.

Capital's approach to portfolio management uses multiple managers; the organization, not individuals, manages assets. We will tell clients which managers manage their particular assets, but we will not tell them the proportions handled or the returns achieved by any individual manager. Currently, each fund in our system is managed by 3–10 portfolio managers; one fund is a research portfolio that is essentially equivalent to one of our fully diversified portfolios but has 15 or 16 participating analysts and tends to be larger. This approach is not new; our multiple-manager system was originally instituted in the late 1950s to deal with concerns about size and complexity, and it was augmented with the research portfolio in the mid-1960s.

One major benefit from our system is clear, at least to us: If a portfolio manager leaves the firm, then only a small chunk (much less than 25 percent) of the assets managed is affected. Furthermore, the other portfolio managers and analysts will already be familiar with all the stocks in the portfolio; thus, portfolio security turnover can be greatly reduced. This approach imparts a modular quality to the system that allows us to drop in a new experienced portfolio manager if an existing portfolio manager departs or if a fund or account grows rapidly. The multimanager system allows us to preserve most of the factors that produced the historical record that the clients evaluated and that, hopefully, will produce the record they expect in the future.

Reward Systems That Maximize Results

When a firm creates any investment system, particularly a multimanager system, it must focus on the requirements that accompany such a system. Those requirements include hiring a diverse group of individuals (if these individuals are not different, then why have multiple managers?), designing an environment that encourages collaboration and cooperation, and putting together compensation and reward systems with multiple elements or layers that emphasize both individual achievement and collaboration and cooperation.

None of this discussion should suggest that we do not hire highly competitive, aggressive risk takers; we do. But to maximize results and collaboration, we structure our organization so that competition is channeled outside the organization against the markets and our competitors rather than among our managers. This channeling is largely done through the measurement and reward system. If a firm wants fairness, generosity, and commitment organizationally, then the top of the organization must show the way. I learned this lesson early in my career at Capital. When I was first offered the opportunity to buy some stock in Capital, I was excited, and I bought the stock. Little did I know in 1973 that we were about to enter a very difficult investment period; it was one of the few times in my experience that the value of Capital stock, which is determined by a formula price, actually declined significantly in the following 1[illegible] months. Being a brash young analyst at the time, I went to the research director and said, "It would be wonderful if you would give me the opportunity to buy some more stock and average down." A few weeks later, the chief financial officer walked into my office and offered me an amount of stock equivalent to my first purchase but at the lower price; the stock was sold to me by the then president of the company and the son of the founder. The lesson: Fairness, generosity, and commitment must come from the top of the organization.

Today, many of us who have management positions are trying to show our fairness, generosity, and commitment to those farther down in the organization. We structure multiple levels of bonuses and rewards. We reward individual achievement and then we add another layer of compensation based on the results of the whole organization similar to a profit-sharing plan. Finally, we have a third level of reward—ownership—which is again based on the achievements of the whole.

We measure results against market indexes and against competitive indexes but never against each other. Consistently superior long-term investment returns define success from our perspective. For example, the investment bonus pool for a portfolio manager is simply defined as outperforming, on a four-year basis, whatever the appropriate benchmark is. We try to structure the benchmarks to be reasonable proxies for the environment in which a person is working—U.S., non-U.S., global, or small-capitalization, for instance; different benchmarks are used for different portfolios. A similar process applies to analysts who are measured against a customized benchmark composed of a specific set of companies or, sometimes, industries.

We spend countless hours on benchmarks, measurement systems, and evaluations to ensure that they are as fair and realistic as possible. The overriding theme is objectivity. We define individual responsibilities (for analysts and portfolio managers) so that they can be fairly measured, and we use those measurements as a basis for paying bonuses. We create bonus pools that are expandable as firm performance increases instead of "fixed pies"; hence, we reduce an individual's focus on maximizing "my slice of the pie" at the expense of someone else's.

The proportion of a person's compensation composed of salary, bonus, profit sharing, and ownership relates to the length of time the person has been with the organization. Senior individuals, including portfolio managers, receive a substantial portion (over half) of their total compensation from ownership and profit sharing. In an analyst's first few years, more than half of the total compensation can come from bonuses through a complex measurement process. Each analyst manages a pool of money, and we measure that pool exactly as we measure results for a portfolio manager. These measurements are one component of an analyst's bonus. The other component of an analyst's bonus attempts to assess the quality of the research job that the analyst did in the period of time evaluated.

Nonmonetary factors are also important. We try to balance individual achievement, cooperation, collaboration, and overall contribution. We try to avoid popularity contests. We maintain an eternal fight against the inevitable creep of structure and bureaucracy because these very talented people do not like structure and bureaucracy. We hope that this structure allows our investment professionals to focus on what they do best. We try to build jobs around what individuals want to do rather than create job descriptions and fill them.

Star versus Team Approaches: A Critical Look

Many organizations have developed, and apparently successfully so, along a model that we call the star system, which is often identified with one portfolio manager for each portfolio. Some firms are created by stars. Ironically, a lot of the success of Capital from 1933 to the mid-1950s (pre-multimanager days) was built around the performance and record of a portfolio predominantly run by one individual. Not all organizations began with stars, but many of them have been built on the shoulders of one star or another and then gone on to modify their approaches to accommodate growth and size.

The star system is crisp and clear, but it depends on the stars in the constellation to deliver. Our concerns about that approach are many. The star system invites some compelling rhetorical questions: How many true stars are there in the investment world? Does their success in asset growth eventually dim their brightness and brilliance?

We also worry about some specific issues inherent in the star system. First, to build a business around a star or two can often lead to a wide range of results among clients. Should we take on a client under the stipulation that only a specific individual manages that client's account? What if that individual leaves? How do we explain that account assignment to other clients? Second, most stars have, in fact, achieved significant investment results, but frequently, the media or other organizations will use those investment results to help create the stars. The great risk for investors is not understanding why the star was successful, which creates the real possibility of "throwing money" at the star at a time when he or she has already peaked. Finally, what kind of work environment does the star system create? Can we be fair to a broad group of talented people in a culture that creates stars, allows and encourages them to burn brightly, and permits them to overshadow many excellent people who, by the nature of the star system, become supporting characters?

Our answer is no. Capital has very few stars that anyone would recognize. Only one or two individuals get much press coverage, which is all part of our effort to promote teamwork and cooperation. Almost by definition, the multiple-portfolio manager system works against star creation. The star "syndrome" will probably be around forever, whether it is in sports or investing, but we can never know who on the team will help us most at any time. Stars are always dangerous, in the sense that a focus on them may overshadow the valuable contributions of others.

We may have disclaimed the star system, but in truth, our system does have its own problems and potential drawbacks. First, it is hard to bring others from the outside into Capital without some considerable culture shock. To try to manage that shock better, we use a detailed and exhaustive, some would say inordinately cumbersome, interviewing and hiring process in which a candidate goes through four or five rounds of interviews, meets 12–15 individuals, and is voted on by everyone. As Parker Hall mentioned, part of the interviewing objective is re-enforcing the notion that we need to find not only good people but people who fit with the broad array of personalities and systems that we have.[2] After going through that interview process, the individual comes in with a sense of having had a real chance to look at this organization. The challenge with young people is that they do not believe how much autonomy they will have. During the first year, young people often wonder, "Where are the people who are supposed to tell me what I should be doing?" With experienced people, the challenge is realizing and coming to grips with the fact that we mean what we say: Capital is a collegial workplace that offers many opportunities to contribute, an enormous amount of freedom, and a fair environment. Sometimes people take a long time to adjust to this atmosphere.

A second potential disadvantage of our system is that the client or shareholder will never experience the best work of one individual when she or he is "hot": Clients get a blend of results from several individuals. Our system works to reduce volatility, to smooth results. If all the portfolio managers are long-term outperformers, we will produce consistently superior long-term investment results. Although many people may scoff at our goals, achieving 150–200 basis points above a benchmark over 10, 15, or 20 years is a heroic achievement in this business.

Ironically, a related concern is that, although overall results are smoothed by our system, individual portfolio managers' returns can be quite dispersed in a given year. In a year when one person has superior returns and another person underperforms, a 1,000 basis point difference can easily exist between the two individuals. One advantage of a multimanager system is that the individual portfolios can be more focused on high-conviction ideas. Therefore, individual portfolios can have both greater volatility and a greater chance of outperforming. Diversification in an account, lower volatility, and the smoothing of results is achieved by mixing the individual portfolios. Substantial differences can and often do exist among the results of individual portfolios before they are amalgamated into the whole.

Another set of issues revolves around the extent to which investment decisions are made "collaboratively" versus "individually" by the managers responsible for a fund or account. For example, a question often arises about how we should deal with the conflict when two managers are buying and selling the same stock in a given portfolio or when different analysts have different opinions on the same stock. We assume that if managers are going to be measured and compensated according to the results they achieve, they have to make their own decisions, but a lot of collaborative discussion, jawboning, and debate between individuals takes place. We do have an investment control process to monitor the situation in which one manager wants to buy a stock and another wants to sell the same stock. The first portfolio manager would buy the stock from the other portfolio manager in the system. We would only go outside the firm if no one internally wanted to buy the stock that the other individual was trying to sell. This internal investment control process makes the entire portfolio management process somewhat slower, but loss of a day or two is not so important when portfolios turn over on average 25–30 percent a year.

Client contact issues must also be addressed. In our system, the client sees one portfolio, which is an amalgam of the different subportfolios beneath it. Each client account and each mutual fund has a lead portfolio manager. That lead person is the one who looks at the portfolio as a whole like a client would. The lead person may talk to a client more regularly than the others involved with the portfolio, but the client will probably meet them all over time. Institutional clients in particular want to see the investment professionals, but we would love to find a way to reduce that involvement for many of our people. Some of them thrive on it; some do not. This is a prime example of trying to identify people's strengths and focusing on getting them to spend time doing what they do well.

Finally, consultants and plan sponsors, particularly those in the institutional world, struggle with

[2]See Mr. Hall's presentation, pp. 20–22.

understanding our system. Many do not like the complexity of our system, nor are they happy if and when they cannot meet the portfolio manager who manages their assets. We sometimes struggle with the system, which is complex and highly computer intensive. It requires considerable management time and effort to identify and solve issues of fairness. The system does not easily lend itself to simple explanations, nor to black-and-white answers to questions concerning measurement.

So, a critical look at star (as practiced at some firms) and team (as practiced at Capital) approaches reveals that both have strengths and weaknesses; the choice, and any resolution of the debate for an individual firm, must go back to the firm's goals, culture, and unique strengths and resources. The debate as an absolute proposition is rather pointless.

Conclusion

Neither Capital's team-based approach nor another firm's star-based system is necessarily right for all organizations; every organization presents the opportunity for a custom-designed management approach. Even our own processes are constantly adjusted, tweaked, and altered. If we have not had a significant organizational adjustment in about three years, we know one is right around the corner. Basic values are more or less constant, but structures need to be adapted and evaluation systems need to be modified. We are always asking a broad group of our people what they want to do. We want to capture their changing sense of passion and the nuances as they develop, and we want to create opportunities and challenges that meet their needs and expectations. Organizational structure is more a process than a monument, and that flexibility is essential to permit individuals to be creative. In fact, we need to battle for change because many obstacles to change (i.e., many preservers of the status quo) exist. Change is good and powerful and allows us to move toward our goals and our fantasies.

Question and Answer Session

James Rothenberg, CFA

Question: Because bonuses are tied to the performance of the whole portfolio, how do you deal with underperformers who may negatively affect the compensation of individuals who are consistently outperforming?

Rothenberg: As a portfolio manager, you may have several different portfolio responsibilities in different portfolio accounts in the institutional business, but the performance results that you are evaluated against are your own, not those of the overall client portfolios. Somebody else's negative results do not affect what you can earn on performance-based bonuses.

On the other hand, negative results do affect the overall return and potentially influence the profitability of the organization, the profit-sharing plan, and over time, total compensation. All of our measurement systems are based on four-year rolling averages. The averages are weighted 40, 30, 20, and 10 percent each year, respectively, rolling years forward as we go along. The long-term contributions in investment returns and broad contributions to the organization are factored into an individual's share of the profit-sharing pool and stock ownership. So, underperformance can have a negative impact. Our focus in such a case is on how to help the underperformer because all of us have gone through periods of time when we have underperformed. We try to keep our compensation practices focused on the long term.

Question: When determining compensation, do you use risk-adjusted returns or nominal returns?

Rothenberg: We do not use risk-adjusted returns, partly because the risks that we focus on are business risks. Whether a company will be able to compete is different from assessing the volatility of a stock using measures such as standard deviation. We focus on nominal returns measured against predetermined benchmarks.

Question: Should top managers play a "hands on" role in portfolio management?

Rothenberg: From my perspective, a majority of the top managers in the organization need to be active investment professionals. If we define our mission as providing consistently superior long-term investment results, then we want to be sure that our business decisions allow us to fulfill our mission. The only way to truly do that is to have the people who are active in the investment process spend a great deal of time in the business discussions.

Question: How do you allocate stock from a small initial public offering (IPO) when several managers want the stock?

Rothenberg: First, we identify an IPO that we are truly interested in owning. Our strategy is not to participate in everything and then sell quickly, although we certainly do take advantage of short-term mispricing when we see it. The allocation question is frequently solved by the fact that we have a small-capitalization fund in our institutional business; many of the IPOs are from small companies and thus go into the small-cap fund, which many of the clients participate in. This solution avoids the question of everything going to one client or another.

In terms of portfolio managers, we have learned over time that a cooperative stance works best: "You take this one, and I will take that one." In a hot IPO environment, no one is going to get a lot of shares anyway. Collegiality and teamwork serve us well in this situation.

Question: Can analysts or portfolio managers buy stocks that are owned in the firm's accounts for their own personal accounts?

Rothenberg: We have always had a very strict approach to this issue. We have a committee that handles all requests for exceptions from investment professionals or anyone else who has any knowledge of our transactions. If we are active in a security, it is very difficult for individuals to buy that security for their personal accounts. Although I agree with the stance that we have taken, I should emphasize that we are not trying to discourage investment. This is an investment business, and when you hire people in the investment business, you want people who are hungry to invest; so, there is a real trade-off. The stricter you are, the more you squelch creativity. We always try to ask ourselves: What is it going to look like if it appears in *The Wall Street Journal*? This question defines our approach and decisions pretty well.

Question: Would you rather deal with a sell-side research firm built on star individual analysts or on overall quality?

Rothenberg: When Wall Street people get to be stars, they are n as useful to us as when they were spending most of their time doing research. On the other hand, some of our people, because they have worked together with some of Wall Street's brightest stars for a long period of time, have established wonderful working relationships with those stars. But those personal relationships are what drive the effectiveness of our interactions with those stars. My advice to young analysts is: Do not pay attention to the stars. Find the young people who have been around one to three years, who are trying to make a name for themselves, and who are still spending 80–90 percent of their time actually doing work in the field. Those are the people with whom you want to interact, the people who are closest to the information you need, and the group from which the next stars will emerge.

Leading Investment Professionals: A Team Approach

J. Parker Hall III, CFA
President and Managing Director
Lincoln Capital Management Company

Management and leadership fads come and go, but important lessons can be learned from firms that follow a consistent investment approach. Lincoln Capital Management's experience has been driven by a focus on four key areas of investment firm leadership: investment philosophy, investment process, returns, and compensation.

New management and leadership approaches, touted as the latest "can't miss fix," are constantly showing up; many firms are quick to adopt and just as quick to jettison a "fix" once the new approach is found wanting. Often, the best lessons for management and leadership are learned by observing firms that have chosen a particular philosophy, structure, and style and have stayed the course over a long time frame. This presentation reviews the experience, specifically on the equity side, of Lincoln Capital Management with respect to four key areas of investment firm leadership: philosophy, process, returns, and compensation.

Lincoln Capital Management

Lincoln has 10 investment professionals (8 research analysts and 2 portfolio managers), 42 clients, and roughly $13 billion in assets under management. (Our bond segment, although not discussed here, has about $25 billion in assets for 70 clients.) Like most investment organizations, our business objective is to satisfy our clients fully in terms of portfolio returns and service, and we do everything toward this end.

Philosophy

Lincoln is a large-capitalization growth manager. We purposefully define our investment philosophy rather narrowly to concentrate our energy and experience. I used to think that growth stock investing suffered from a steady head wind. We have all read about how value stocks outperform growt stocks, small-cap growth stocks outperform large cap growth stocks, and foreign stocks outperform domestic stocks. For the past 10 years, howeve value has not outperformed growth. For the past 1 years, small-cap growth has not outperforme large-cap growth. For the past 20 years, foreig stocks ex-Japan and in local currency have not ou performed domestic stocks. Additionally, relativ P/Es and yields of large-cap growth stocks ar more attractive presently than a decade ago. So, large-cap universe appears to be representativel populated with attractive investment candidates.

Process

To implement our narrow investment philosoph Lincoln uses a rather traditional investment proce with a heavy emphasis on field work. Our eig research analysts, each of whom has had at least years of industry or investment experience befo joining Lincoln, have specific industry assignmen and follow about 30 stocks each. We try hard know enough about the companies we follow th we can be willing to hold, or indeed buy, wh near-term prospects are daunting (albeit temp rarily, we hope). We talk a lot together, both info mally and in a formal decision-making mode. used to worry that multifactor models, index fund or other creative approaches to investing wou make the more traditional hands-on approach obs lete, but I do not worry about that much any mor Organizations that are quantitatively oriented not seem to have systematically superior returns.

We have essentially used the same valuation discipline for more than 25 years: relative P/Es. The system that a firm uses does not matter, however, as long as it is reasonable and pursued consistently. Our process has been modified and enhanced, and it appears to be fruitful because transactions usually add value to the portfolios. We are also becoming increasingly involved in economic value analysis, an approach that seems to be useful in judging the productivity of companies' capital investments over time. A valuable by-product of our valuation approach is that it has permitted our conversations with company managers to focus on the long term, beyond the next quarter or next year.

One somewhat nontraditional aspect of Lincoln's investment process is that we do not have portfolio managers in the usual sense. We make investment decisions as a team. Any of the 10 investment professionals can initiate a recommendation. This approach leads to discussion and, usually, to an immediate decision. We follow Roberts' Rules of Order: Each of us present has one vote, and the majority carries. This arrangement has four advantages:

- Each equity person is an integral part of the team. Each has a full vote and is expected to use it responsibly.
- Each researcher participates fully in the construction of the portfolio, which everyone likes. Researchers can usually make something happen on their assigned stocks. Individually and collectively, we try to help our associates. All of us have come to appreciate this horizontal rather than hierarchical structure.
- We are not immobilized or restrained by committees and quorums. As few as one person can make a portfolio decision, although we more often have four to eight participating. Implementation of a decision usually starts immediately.
- Our client portfolios are nearly identical, which is a natural extension of this focus on one investment philosophy and shared decision making. We believe that clients with similar objectives deserve similar portfolios—the best a firm can create. Dispersion of returns is appropriately narrow. Our clients do not worry about which portfolio manager is assigned to them or about annual compensation arrangements that often contribute to people pulling apart rather than pulling together.

Another aspect of the process is that the two equity portfolio people share all of the client assignments and participate fully in investment decisions. On their own responsibility, they almost never implement a transaction that touches on all portfolios. They assure that specific client guidelines are met and that communications are effective. A long-term perspective is at least partially reflected in Lincoln's equity portfolio turnover, which averages 33 percent annually. Turnover is also a function of the character of the portfolio companies (fairly stable businesses), our knowledge of them, and the implementation of our valuation discipline.

In terms of clients, Lincoln has exercised restraint in pursuing growth. Our goal has been to add one or two new equity clients annually, a pace that we have averaged for the past decade. The benefit of this modest growth is that we retain the character of a more intimate boutique without marketing, without a head of research, without a large group of portfolio managers, and without a large infrastructure.

Finally, the way we recruit investment professionals also reflects our investment process and focus. We let other firms train analysts, and even within that context, we try to obtain the services of recognized, outstanding researchers. We look for people the same way we look for stocks and make decisions; we take a horizontal approach. Our own analysts are the principal people conducting the interviews because we are hiring somebody who is going to work with them. The last person we hired was selected after roughly nine months. Each of our analysts traveled to the city in which that analyst was living to get to know that person.

For us, hiring the right person is crucial because analysts who join Lincoln are no longer in the public domain in terms of potential stardom. They no longer have audiences that are in awe of them, simply associates who hold them in great esteem. When they join Lincoln, they are going to have to live a long and comfortable life doing mostly what they are doing.

Returns

Lincoln is a strong proponent of good benchmarking. We have used a well-specified custom benchmark for more than a decade. This growth benchmark was developed because at the time, unlike now, good style standards did not exist in the public domain. Now, lots of appropriate benchmarks exist. We know what bets we are making relative to the benchmarks, both overweighting and underweighting. We receive monthly performance reports, detailed by analyst, with all the subsectors displayed by both selection and sector return attribution. Our firm's principal strength is in individual stock selection, and accordingly, we heavily weight our favorite stocks.

Despite appropriately structured benchmarks, our relative returns have ebbed and flowed, as is the nature of our business. For instance, we materially lagged in 1973, 1983, and 1993: We have alerted our clients to beware of 2003. With respect to AIMR-compliant equity returns, however, data for periods ending February 29, 1996, show us ahead of growth standards for all 24 cumulative periods starting in 1972 with an average excess return of more than 2 percent annually.

Compensation

Despite having what we think are very good performance diagnostics for compensation purposes, we tend to think in periods of three years or longer—perhaps a more extended time frame than is used by most institutional sponsors. We allocate revenues of the firm partly based on a compensation pool and partly based on ownership. Because short periods are too loaded with static and random good and bad luck, we pay no annual bonuses to investment professionals. Once the calendar year starts, each person's compensation depends entirely on the firm's income or, basically, how our clients are doing. Once-a-year judgments about each equity person's share of compensation are based on long-term considerations. These factors include several years' returns relative to a specific benchmark and also potential for professional growth, overall contribution to our decision making, collaboration, congeniality, and hard work.

At Lincoln, equity ownership usually comes within a new investment professional's first year. We think good people should be able to become a shareholder fairly promptly so that they identify immediately with what is going on in the company. A substantial portion of the firm's revenues are allocated to shareholder interests; therefore, buyers get a good return on the stock. We do not require anybody to buy stock, but our experience is that they do step up and buy it, either paying cash or assuming notes. The transfer price is material, but it is less than that available in the public market for investment management firms. This transfer price reflects the fact that we are private, the buyer owns a minority interest, and the firm is not broadly diversified. A person who has been at Lincoln for a decade or more has accumulated significant savings and equity, so the urge to merge in order to maximize immediate wealth is subdued. Presently, we have about 20 shareholders.

Our expectation for an investment professional at Lincoln is a long-term and mutually satisfying relationship. We think of the relationship as no less than a marriage. Not many substantial firms exist any more that are completely independent. Being private does not assure fulfillment of client expectations, but it does help concentrate a manager's attention on the portfolio and the client. For instance, we are especially sensitive about even the appearance of potential conflicts with client interests, including use of our time. One reflection of this belief is that no employee can purchase any stock in our benchmark.

Conclusion

Has the Lincoln approach to management and leadership worked? With respect to investment professionals, only two—one equity and one bond—have left Lincoln for reasons other than retirement during the past 20 years. With respect to returns, we have met most client objectives. No client has left Lincoln for at least a decade because of disappointment over returns, and nearly one-half of our 42 clients have been with us for more than 10 years. Many factors may have been and likely were at work in these results, but no matter how an investment firm measures success, investment philosophy and process, compensation, and returns clearly have played an important role at Lincoln.

Leading Investment Professionals: Start with Fundamentals

Claude N. Rosenberg, Jr.
Principal
RCM Capital Management

The way to lead investment professionals may seem obvious: Find the right people, who will have staying power, for the right firm. Attention to certain fundamentals, however—the hiring process, the stance of the manager, effective work habits, discipline, and creativity—may well raise the quality of leadership.

The key to leading investment professionals—portfolio managers, research analysts, and even people involved in marketing—may well be as simple, or as difficult, as finding the right people for the particular firm: people who will have staying power in this volatile business. Attention to certain fundamentals, however, can raise the level of leadership; this presentation discusses the importance of several fundamental factors: the hiring process, the stance of the manager, effective work habits, discipline, and creativity.

Hiring

The starting point in managing a firm is to make sure the right people are hired. Learning as much as possible about an interviewee before he or she joins the firm is important. One often overlooked question is whether a person, particularly one who has not been in the investment industry, has the staying power within the industry. I try to describe for that person what it is like to live through a bear market, when people in the investment business must assume that, for a couple of years, almost everything they own will be on a downward slant. Contrary to the 1975–95 period, prolonged down markets do happen. As wonderful as this business is, offering such great opportunities for creativity and stimulation, it is not easy to be a part of these "down times." We all have to find a way to make it through those times; after all, we are dealing in the stock market, which has great liquidity but also portends great volatility. Even in the better markets, not all of us succeed as we would wish, as daily stock price quotes remind us. Describing these situations for people is important because at RCM, to put it candidly, we do not want people in the organization who cannot stand the heat and yet want to stay in the kitchen.

Managerial Stance

Empathy and humility are required for properly managing people in the investment management industry. Mistakes are inevitable, and the newspapers remind us daily of those mistakes. Supervisors must know how to react to those mistakes and to the people who make them. Managers should ask their staff: If you are wrong, what went wrong? Was it the fundamentals of the stock or the market in general that was different from what you were anticipating? Were you wrong for a reason that could have been foreseen? The same basic questions should also be asked when someone is right. When we judge our employees' performance, determining whether they are correct for the right or the wrong reasons is important; giving plaudits for things that are luck does not make sense.

Regardless of the type of decision made, I like to ask people: "What would you have done differently?" I try to understand the people on the other side of my desk who are going through a difficult time, whether they have misjudged the market (probably not their assigned responsibility anyway) or they have made the wrong choice in an industry or individual stock. If we are going to help people, we have to work hard at it, be good listeners, and be proactive. We have to probe intelligently, try to help our employees along, and get them to realize that we all make mistakes and the best thing to do is benefit from the mistakes.

Work Habits

Something as simple as encouraging and displaying effective work habits goes a long way in raising the level of leadership. The realm of the research analyst provides many rich examples of such leadership.

■ *Be prepared.* One secret to success, for instance, is good preparation. I remember spending many hours as a security investment analyst trying to determine what I had overlooked and what kind of preparation I could make that would hold me in better stead during an interview with an officer of a company being analyzed.

■ *Set priorities.* Along with preparation goes the ability to set and stick to priorities. Analysts seldom get as much time with the corporate representatives they are interviewing as they think they should have, so they must prioritize and know what answers are absolutely necessary to take away from that meeting. A good example of sticking to priorities is to make sure that the company's "dog-and-pony show" does not usurp that valuable, limited research time.

■ *Ask impertinent questions.* The willingness to ask the impertinent questions—the questions that a company does not want to face and may not be overly willing to answer but that are key to the analyst's understanding of the company—is critical. Analysts must isolate their perceived negatives and probe to determine whether management is aware of them—and what specifically, if anything, management plans to do about them.

■ *Analyze the analyses of others.* Finally, encouraging people to analyze the analyses of others is important. Analysts should try to find out how other people make their decisions and whether they make correct ones. A few years ago, for example, I set out to learn how decision makers in real estate decided whether they should buy or sell properties and how the price levels were determined. I found that their key assumptions on vacancy rates, tenant improvement costs, and new rentals were extremely negative—so negative that I did not have to be a real estate expert to pick the bottom of the real estate market. I have found that the people who are closest to any asset that has been "bombarded" typically lose perspective near the bottom. By knowing how evaluations are determined, this "lack of perspective" hypothesis can be tested to determine the strength of an industry or an individual stock.

Discipline

A vital task for managing people is to create whatever discipline is needed to help people along, whether the discipline pertains to investment decisions, effective communications, or objectivity.

■ *Investment discipline.* It may sound silly to state that we at RCM do not want to own stocks about which we have little conviction. This stance is especially true in bad markets, when it is particularly critical to own companies or businesses that we believe in. We want to own stocks that we would own regardless of the markets. So, for example, when initial public offerings (IPOs) are hot, we impose a discipline on ourselves. Some people are willing to jump in if they hear that a stock IPO's per share price is coming to market at $15 but is expected to jump to $30. An effective discipline here would be: Are we willing to buy more of the stock at, say, 10 or 15 percent above the $15 offering price—hence, at $17 or $18? If not, we should not participate at all. If we do participate and the price goes nowhere, we will end up owning a stock that we do not want; not only will we have a bad portfolio, but we will also have a wrenching emotional experience.

Other investment decisions for which discipline is crucial include the amount of cash we are willing to hold and the number of companies owned in any portfolio. Consider the following hypothetical rule: Cash in the portfolio has to be either less than 3 percent or more than 12 percent. This dictum forces "hard" decision making rather than allowing a lot of ups and downs between 3 percent and 12 percent that keep the manager from being fully invested while never forcing enough protection against negative performance. Too many managers swing back and forth from 4 percent to 10 percent in cash with little purpose or conviction. In a similar manner, the number of companies owned should be limited. Placing no limits on the number of companies owned can lead to "closet" indexing at considerably higher fees because it can promote laziness on the part of analysts and portfolio managers. Although no magic number of holdings exists that works for everyone, small accounts should own fewer securities and larger portfolios should own more but should have limits low enough so that every holding is important.

Recognizing when disciplines should change is also important. For example, if our primary discipline is built around P/Es but we believe that cash flow and free cash flow are not given sufficient attention in the market, then we should work to augment, or replace the P/E discipline with extensions that highlight cash flow and free cash flow.

▪ *Communications discipline.* When adding discipline to an organization, an important task is to point out and eliminate the expressions that indicate confusion in the speaker's mind. For example, a suspect expression would be: "I have done the research on this company, and I like the business and the company, but I would like to buy it lower." Of course, we all would like to buy stocks at a lower price. The expression "I would like to buy it lower" suggests "I am afraid I will be wrong; therefore, I am covering myself for later accountability." Another suspect expression is, "I am a buyer at $42, and I am likely to sell some or all at $46 or $47." The speaker is hiding the fact that he or she wants to procrastinate, is not confident of the research, or is simply trying to hide in the corner. To be fair, defining where the responsibility lies for setting buy and sell prices—with people on the analytical side or with portfolio managers—is an important part of a firm's communications discipline. The responsibility could logically rest with either analysts or managers, but the discipline should be clear and clearly communicated.

Another important communications discipline is to be conscious of reading internal memos. I try to read everything that comes from our analytical staff, which totals more than 40 people. When I read those memos, I look for things that are the most interesting, annotate wherever I have (I hope) cogent thoughts and questions, and send the memo back to the writer. This process is good for me because it causes me to concentrate as I go through the memo, and it is good for the writers because they know somebody has read the memo, is paying attention, and responds positively in some way to it.

▪ *Objectivity.* An important goal of discipline is objectivity; an analyst should not be so close to the management in any company that he or she loses objectivity. Friendships are wonderful, but when they interfere with objectivity, then they interfere with the job. I once had a research department head who, if flattered appropriately by the executive that he was interviewing, almost always came to a positive conclusion about the company. I sat down with him and said, "You are too influenced by what they are telling you about your work, and you are not being as objective as you should be." He eventually turned out to be a great analyst but only after having the discipline of objectivity reimposed.

Creativity

One of the most important leadership responsibilities in this tough business is creating excitement, which is probably best done by encouraging creativity and innovation.

At RCM, for instance, we have a "sleuth of the month" award, which has to do with challenging people to be creative and to come to conclusions in innovative ways. If someone has done research or reached conclusions in a manner different from the Street or others, then we should honor that person. We should also let people make mistakes. I have purposely labeled ideas of mine as "Rosenberg's Follies" to indicate that new, even crazy, ideas are worth a try in our organization. If new ideas are ultimately not productive, then our stance is: To err is human. Taking a chance and doing things imaginatively is far better than doing nothing at all.

Such a stance encourages people to find new ways to do things. For instance, at RCM our regular research department, about 30 people in all, has traditional tasks—balance sheet and income statement analysis and talking to the managers of the companies. The research staff is mainly structured by industry responsibility, but we do try to make sure that, whenever possible, people get to see industries with different P/E multiples or price-to-cash-flow characteristics so that they do not get into a rut. To "push the envelope" a bit and to pursue another possible Rosenberg Folly, we decided to create a "Grassroots Research" department of about 12 people—a "get in the field, kick the tires" approach that, in our judgment, the Street does not do well. Our Grassroots Research department does not talk to top management. We want them in the field answering whatever questions we throw at them: Is an individual product doing well? What products or companies are hurting? What are inventory levels? Who is beating whom? We are not peeping through keyholes; we are trying to find ways to determine who is doing a good job and who is not, but not through management's eyes. During the first couple of years, we were concerned that everybody would try to mimic this approach, but after more than 11 years, nobody else has done it.

Giving praise independent of performance is also important, and apparently rare. Patting people on the back when they sink a three-pointer or score the winning touchdown is easy, but the time when people need compliments is when things are drab or difficult. To continue the sports analogy, we should be more aware of giving compliments for a sacrifice fly or a solid defensive play or a stalwart no-decision pitching performance, not merely for home runs or a no-hitter.

Make no mistake about it; monetary praise is important. At RCM, we believe in sharing the wealth through revenue allocations and a bonus pool. We have 19 principals, and one person could conceivably earn as much as 10–12 percent of our profits, although 10 percent would be a more typical figure. Parker Hall's approach to having people buy an equity position in the firm is probably better than what we have used over the years.[1] If we were to do it again, I would make sure people did put up more money along the way, both to show their confidence in the institution itself and to position themselves for greater rewards long term.

One common reward-related problem that we have not had to address, and probably will not have to, is that of compensation differentials between stars and good team players. RCM is not a star-system firm. Ours is a team process; in our history, we have had only one situation, many years ago, in which a star was involved. All parties ultimately agreed that the fit was poor. I strongly advocate avoiding the star system, which makes a firm vulnerable to that one person's whims or longevity at the firm.

Conclusion

Attention to these leadership fundamentals has served RCM well; on average, our clients have stayed with us for 15 years, which we take to mean that we are producing good performance result and communicating those results effectively. Bein driven by these fundamentals, however, has als allowed us to take on other responsibilities, one o which is overview. That is, when RCM hires you a an equity or fixed-income manager, you have a indirect responsibility to go beyond that very spe cific mission given to you: If something happen that you think is important to your client, yo should make sure you communicate that informa tion. For example, in the early 1970s when we sa inflation coming, we communicated that to our cli ents and stuck our necks out with specific sugge tions on what to do, and we therefore entered th fixed-income business—that is, to keep our client who owned bonds outside our management fro losing money (and they would have lost it i spades had they not followed our advice and shor ened their bond maturities dramatically). Durin the same period, we recommended the ownershi of high-quality, income-producing properties for a cash, which in turn led to our formation of th RREEF (Rosenberg Real Estate Equity Fund) Co poration, which served our clients well for years come. Clients should respect and appreciate yo "sticking your neck out." To me, sticking your ne out is the essence and the importance of a uniq client–manager relationship because it is the sign an empathetic, helpful, well-intentioned manager.

[1]See Mr. Hall's presentation, pp. 20–22.

Question and Answer Session

J. Parker Hall III, CFA
Claude N. Rosenberg, Jr.

Question: Do you have any quantitative methods for measuring an analyst's contribution?

Hall: We use a custom benchmark for each analyst. In fact, the analysts themselves choose the stocks that are in their benchmarks. In this way, we can determine exactly what each analyst's contribution is to the active portfolio. We add up each of the eight analysts' individual contributions, and we get exactly how the total portfolio has done relative to the total benchmark.

Rosenberg: We try not to reward people only for their preceding 12-month contributions; the best approach we have found is to use a 40, 30, 20, and 10 percent allocation, respectively, for what has happened in each of the past four years. With this approach, people know that they will be judged on a long-term basis—not only by a "what have you done for me lately" philosophy.

Question: What is your firm's philosophy toward growth?

Hall: Our philosophy toward growth is related to the addition of 1–2 clients a year, with a base of about 40 clients. We would not have even that kind of growth, except that it feels good to be in an organization that is growing to some degree and is not wholly dependent on the level of the stock or the bond market or the ability to add value, which is more problematic. So, where we can, we grow modestly; most of the time, however, we do not accept new clients.

Rosenberg: Three times in our history we shut off the opportunity to consider prospective clients, the most recent time starting in 1992. We did that because we felt it was time to look at our processes, people, and everything involving our investment decision making on the equity side to see whether we needed to make some fairly important changes, which we did. This period of no growth lasted for more than two-and-a-half years and led to methods that should benefit our clients for years to come.

Question: How much time do you allocate to client relations versus investment/portfolio management? How do your clients like this arrangement?

Rosenberg: Clients used to consider heavy marketing as "suspicious." Not so today. Similarly, client servicing is coming closer to portfolio management. We have formed a separate department to make sure that client servicing is being handled better. We want our portfolio people to be available, within limits, to see clients. When things are tough, you cannot, and should not, restrict portfolio managers from whatever it takes to console and inform clients directly. Clients want to see, and get to know, the people who are pulling the triggers. The other extreme you want to avoid is having the portfolio manager on the road so frequently that he or she is not managing money any more. More institutional clients are accepting the fact that client-service people act as good intermediaries between them and the portfolio manager.

Hall: Part of the answer may be based on the size of the firm and the number of clients in the particular product areas. By limiting the number of clients at Lincoln, we can have line investment people, who participate in everyday decisions, actually service the client. The clients like dealing with a senior line investment person who is participating in the creation of their portfolios. If we had two or three times as many clients, I would adopt an approach similar to that just described by Claude Rosenberg. In that circumstance, I think the clients accept that strategy just as well as our strategy.

Question: How do you create an environment for professional growth and job satisfaction?

Rosenberg: To begin with, reward diligence and creativity. During the past six months, I have had regular open sessions in my office for anything analysts want to bounce off of me. Often, a schism exists between portfolio management and research. Research should be creative and get more attention than it sometimes does. We also need to help and encourage our staff to attend conferences or take educational courses.

Hall: Rewarding creativity is important. Every year or so, one of the analysts at Lincoln comes up with an idea that changes how we do things. For example, one of our analysts who has developed our economic value analysis now conducts seminars on that process. We never know where we are going to find people who are particularly imaginative. Ideas do not always work, but try them.

Managing Investment Research Professionals

Patrick O'Donnell
Managing Director and Chief of Global Equity Research
Putnam Investments

No single key exists to meeting the opportunities, problems, and challenges of managing investment research professionals. Any successful management approach, however, should attend to three crucial tasks—recruiting the right people, developing and challenging those people throughout their careers, and evaluating and compensating them in fair and innovative ways.

Managing investment research professionals, who are among the most creative and "high-powered" people anywhere, is a challenging task in and of itself. New and continuing trends in the business, such as the greater degree of engineering in mutual fund products, the replacement of the star system with team-based approaches, and the worldwide consolidation of the industry, only serve to make the job more interesting. The theme of this presentation is the opportunities, problems, and challenges of managing a relatively large research department; in particular, it deals with three key management tasks—recruiting, developing and challenging, and evaluating and compensating research professionals.

The Research Environment

Putnam's research effort, staffed now by nearly 50 people, supports the management of $135 billion in assets, of which $75 billion is in equity and about two-thirds is in mutual funds. Our goal as a research department is to get the right stocks into the right portfolios at the right time.

When we began to expand the central research operations a few years ago, we had to decide what we wanted to be. Although many people have started their investment careers as analysts, we wanted to get away from thinking of an analyst's position as simply an entry-level job. People should not have to leave the jobs that they are doing well and in which they are making their maximum contribution in order to get more money or better psychological/sociological rewards in the organizati So, we decided that we would have a career track analysts.

Fully one-third of our analysts are senior v presidents, which is a title that had traditiona never been held by anybody but relatively sen portfolio managers, and we now have analysts w make as much money as portfolio managers. have made analysts colleagues. In sum, we enco age our analysts. We always look first interna when we have a portfolio management openi but we do not make it necessary for people to ab don a career track that satisfies them and allo them to make a big contribution to the organizati in order to attain more money or prestige.

In addition to making analysts colleagues w portfolio managers, and central to the investm process, we aim for stability in the research dep ment because we want to build on the grou knowledge about the specified universe of sto that we cover, which is large, always growing, a always changing.

We also decided that we would ground our c porate values in an investment process that w characterized by rigorous fundamental analy Now, nobody admits to *not* doing rigorous fun mental analysis. So, what does it mean in our case

Before we recommend a stock for inclusion i portfolio, we develop a five-year forward model the company's income statement, the cash fl statement, and the balance sheet. We project ea ings, cash flow, and dividends; and then we d variety of present-value analyses of those strea not because we think any magic is associated with either part of this two-part discipline but because, as Claude Rosenberg said, having a discipline and sticking to it is important.[1]

I have managed research analysts for some years, and they can be unruly. Actually, if they are the right ones, they will, as a group, be creatively unruly. Therefore, we must be able to say, "This is what we stand for." Our focus on fundamental analysis is a way of saying, "This is what we do, this is what keeps us together as a group, this is what keeps us from becoming a bunch of individuals operating in an unconsciously scattered way."

In our research environment, and probably in any research environment, at least three management tasks must be carried out successfully: recruiting, developing and challenging, and evaluating and compensating analysts.

Recruiting Analysts

The recruiting process sounds simple: Get the right people at the right time in their careers. Then, with the right people, everything else will follow. I firmly believe in those statements, and we invest what some might consider an inordinate amount of time and energy in the recruiting process, particularly in assessing candidate traits and in interviewing.

Candidate Traits

In our years of recruiting and hiring, we have learned two important lessons that we try to keep in mind. First, the perfect candidate does not exist. Second, never bring anybody in because you think you are going to change that person: develop, yes; enhance skills, yes; fundamentally change, forget it. Expecting that someone will change is not fair to that person; it is a fantasy that will not come true.

With those two caveats in mind, we look at a candidate's academic record, mental ability, ethical values, flexibility and adaptability, and ability to handle conflict, along with a few miscellaneous traits.

- *Academic record.* A candidate's academic record, both the good and the bad grades, can reveal a lot about that person, but this record needs to be scrutinized carefully. Suppose a person received straight A's from a prestigious college, worked for two years at a well-respected Wall Street firm, and went to a high-powered business school, also getting straight A's. Even with these credentials, we cannot be sure how good an analyst this person is going to be because what this person may simply have shown is an extraordinary capacity for adaptation, for memorization, and for figuring out how to manipulate the system. This person may also be brilliant, but consistently high grades are not prima facie evidence of investment ability.

Many of our analysts are late bloomers. They are people whose performance was fair in college but who wish they had done much better. In some cases, they were not accepted by their first choices for graduate school, but they worked extremely hard. They did not think that they knew everything, and they did not think they had any competitive edge except that they were very, very hard workers. I agree with Gary Brinson in that I prefer to hire somebody who is a little bit less intelligent but who has focus, enthusiasm, and humility and who is grateful for the job.[2]

We do not look merely at someone's academic record; we look at the range of courses taken. We actually look for a few bad grades. If a candidate has had a poor grade, that interests us. Did he get a bad grade because he was interested in biochemistry even though he did not know anything about it? Assuming he knew that he would never find out unless he took the course and then he got a C, we admire that C because it shows curiosity. It also shows that he is trying to find out about himself with respect to the world, and he may well have a greater level of maturity for having taken the risk to take the course.

If someone's grade point average does not mean everything to us, a rising trend in grades does. We would rather judge candidates at their best than at their average, assuming their best is their recent self. Sometimes we see people with records that are erratic because they have a certain constructive reluctance to go along with authority, which may well be a productive trait in our environment. With the right management approach, those people frequently do very well.

- *Mental ability.* We look for a combination of abstract thinking and practical, problem-solving skills. These people tend not to be perfectionists but realists, and they can conceptualize well. We look for smart people who are good with numbers. We particularly look for the ability to do numbers in one's head, as opposed to using pencil and paper. So much of what we do is by telephone or in conversation that we need the ability to deal with numbers reasonably quickly.

We are looking for people who understand relationships of whole to part and part to whole, so we do some puzzle-solving exercises with them.

[1]See Mr. Rosenberg's presentation, pp. 23–26.

[2]See Mr. Brinson's presentation, pp. 4–7.

We are looking for creative intelligence rather than adaptive intelligence. In the interview, for instance, interesting candidates may choose to present resumés that are not in their business schools' standard formats but are actually arranged in the order that they think is the right way to present themselves; so, they might place work experience before school experience.

- *Ethical values.* We must focus on moral sensibility in our search for new hires. We are fiduciaries, which is the most important aspect of what we do. If someone walked into our research department and asked the first person, "What is the most important thing about what you do?" we hope that person would say, "I am a fiduciary." We are Putnam; Judge Putnam, in 1830, defined the Prudent Person Rule. We take it seriously, and all analysts have a copy of that rule on their walls. We all must remember that we are dealing with real people, real money, and real consequences of our actions.

People have trusted us with their money just as they have trusted their lawyers with their legal affairs. Thus, we look for evidence of altruism in a candidate or a capacity to think about other people.

- *Flexibility and adaptability.* We look for people who have been through something in their lives, particularly a failure, that has required adapting to a situation. Some of our best analysts have experienced some real failures before they got to us, which we think is great preparation.

One of our most successful analysts started and ran a business that did not prosper. He dealt with the failure constructively, and now he has a whole different way of approaching situations. So, we are always looking for some evidence that not everything has gone right and that the person has reacted well to it because, as Rosenberg said, this is a tough business and things do not always go well.

When all of the magic thinking does not work and the stocks go down day after day after day, how much responsibility someone takes on and how articulate that person is, particularly under stress, become important issues.

We often look for people who have had a lot of success in something, but it does not have to be academic success. Two of the best analysts I ever trained were competitive horseback riders. They had the following characteristic: They could do the same thing again and again until they got it right. They had made huge sacrifices elsewhere in their lives in order to be world-class equestrians, and they were very coachable. They wanted to learn. If told that they were doing something in a less-than-optimal way, they would try to do better.

So, we are looking for people who have done something at a very high level of accomplishment. It does not have to be intellectual, but it is best if it involves some sort of sacrifice elsewhere in their lives. If investment management is going to be their profession, something else is going to have to give.

- *Ability to handle conflict.* We are interested in people who are able to handle disagreement. A portfolio manager may own $400 million of some stock that an analyst wants to sell. There will be times when the analyst should expect, and will receive, negative reactions from his or her recommendation. That is human nature, and that is not going to change. Conflict will always exist, so we look for the capacity to operate within a discipline without being doctrinaire. We are also skeptical about people who tend to see things in black and white. Conviction is one thing, but black-and-white thinking is another.

- *Miscellaneous traits.* We enjoy people who exhibit a childish glee when making money in stocks. It sounds obvious, but we like to get people to talk about their early successes with stocks and how their approaches worked. Also, we consider whether people have, for some reason or other, been outsiders in some set of circumstances; that experience has probably made them resourceful and given them focus.

The Interviewing Process

Successful recruiting in general, and interviewing in particular, recognizes two realities. First, an effective research group has to be self-creating. That is, when new colleagues come in, we want the analysts to say, "They are here because I wanted them here" or "They have come in because I was casting a critical vote." Success has many parents. We want broad sponsorship of the new people who enter the department. I would not dream of going to a business school, interviewing some people, making some offers, and then introducing people to their new colleagues. If 15 people interview the candidate, we get a much better perspective and much broader acceptance of the new colleague.

The second realization is that recruiting and interviewing are inherently inefficient processes. Recruiting the right people involves all kinds of work that later is going to look as though it was not productive. We might interview 7–10 candidates before we even get somebody into a finalist position. Our interviewing process is extremely extensive. We do not try to make hiring a fast process. We do try to make it a process that involves the largest number of people who want to be involved; all analysts in the department are allowed to interview every single candidate if they want to. One of the things I believe about this business is that, to some degree, we all come to work each day to make each other smarter or to acknowledge that we need each other's skills. This sentiment is especially true for recruiting.

Because of our approach to interviewing, we give a lot of weight to outlying opinions. If one interviewer has serious reservations about a candidate, we tend to give those reservations a disproportionately large weight in our ultimate decision. This approach may not be the perfect way to hire someone, but having a group that can function well together is absolutely essential. We have probably lost candidates for reasons that were arguable but that were the right decision from the standpoint of producing consistent, long-term investment results for the people who trust us with their money.

Not only do we encourage anyone within the research department to interview candidates, we want the candidates to see anyone they want to. Our best candidates now are so sophisticated about using data-base searching capabilities that they know who is at our organization, what we have done, who manages what, and all sorts of details. We try to keep the door open. Candidates can "kick any tire" in this large organization, and a surprising number of them take us up on it. Needless to say, we like that approach. This is the way we want them to behave when they are analyzing companies and their managements.

Candidates are investing a great deal of their time in the decision they are about to make, and the care that they bring to the process is something that we look at from the very beginning. For example, candidates who do not wait for their schools to get in touch with us but instead set up their own interview schedules are at a competitive advantage. When they are analysts, we do not want them to wait for management to invite them to come for a visit or wait for an industry conference a month away. We want them to call the company and get there soon and try to get a competitive edge. Therefore, somebody who applies at our firm in August gets a better place in the queue than someone who applies with the rest of the herd through the placement office later in the year.

Our candidates go through a series of tests and interviews with psychological professionals who are well-versed in our business. But before we hear any of the results from the testing and the interviewing, the candidates get the results. They are always given time to sit with the testers and, if they so desire, learn what they can about themselves. The extent to which they try to figure out what they could be doing better and where their blind spots are only helps us. In other words, we are watching the entire process, and candidates who show curiosity about how they can better themselves and what they could learn faster impress us.

Finally, after interviewing, we always try to get back to the candidates quickly. We do not keep people waiting. We want them to know at all times their status, partly because keeping them informed gives them a message about how they will be treated when they get to the firm. We do not want candidates to hang in ambiguity wondering why we cannot make up our minds. If we do not have an answer yet, we tell them that, and we tell them when we will know.

Also, we never give anybody a deadline. If we are recruiting a very smart person and say, "We would love to have you work here because you have such good judgment, but we would like you to decide by Thursday at 3:00 p.m.," we are delivering a mixed message. A lot of other people want to talk to the candidates and persuade them to join their organizations. We do not try to persuade them. We show them what we do; we invite them to investment meetings; we let them meet and talk to anybody; but we do not give them a deadline. Instead, we tell them to talk to everybody else because if they come here, we want this to be their professional heart's desire.

This approach does not always make planning easy, but we want candidates to join our firm because they want to, not because they had to make a decision before they heard from somebody else. Our attitude gives us a competitive advantage with the people who are thoughtful.

Recruiting Results

What results do we hope for? When this recruiting process is complete, we hope to have a group that is smart and creative, has little tolerance for bureaucracy, probably has less-than-the-national-average respect for authority, possibly has slightly more-than-the-national-average level of intellectual vanity, and thrives in a business in which there is a high error rate. The end result is that we have a group that varies widely in personality and style. For those of us who like to manage people, this outcome is about as good as it gets; those who do not like to manage people are probably better off on the money management side.

Finally, those who are going to manage people, such as the group I just described, certainly need a management structure that accommodates these individuals—a structure that develops and challenges analysts and one that provides for appropriate evaluation and compensation.

Developing and Challenging Analysts

Developing and challenging analysts is rife with difficulties, but two particular issues stand out. First, development is not something that is limited to new people or to young beginners. Development should take place throughout a career, and opportunities for development and challenge must somehow be made never ending.

The bigger obstacle we face, however, as managers of creative people, is that nearly irresistible forces for conformity exist. Everybody studied essentially the same books; wisdom is all pretty much the same; and the way to get ahead is roughly the same. By going through the accepted procedures and becoming members of the establishment, people tend to have fairly standard qualifications.

Overlay that scenario with the agency problem of managing other people's money and the pressures of losing business if a consultant or corporate treasurer thinks we did something stupid and the result is what John Maynard Keynes asserted: "Worldly wisdom teaches that it is better for reputation to fail conventionally than to succeed unconventionally."[3] So, whatever we do to develop and challenge research professionals has to provide continuing opportunities for our people and has to overcome the inertia of conformity and risk aversion. Our experience suggests several avenues to reach these lofty goals.

Training New Recruits

Part of our training for new analysts is to have the more experienced analysts work directly with the starting analysts. An analyst in most industries cannot cover more than roughly 30 companies at a time with the degree of detail and rigor that we expect, so this process helps both the experienced and new analysts alike. Most senior analysts have some discrete part of the stock universe they follow that can be conveniently broken off and given to a new person. The new analyst can ask the experienced analyst challenging questions and bring fresh eyes to a situation. As a consequence of this process, we are surprised at how often we learn new things about companies we thought we understood well. When the new analysts are ready to go off on their own (sometimes it is weeks, sometimes it is months), they are fully responsible for the investment results in the stocks that we have assigned them. In this way, authority and responsibility are never disentangled. Someone who has the responsibility also has the authority, but it is nice to know that somebody with experience is able to help if needed. Once the new analysts become experienced, they break in the next generation of analysts. We know that this model for training is not traditional, but we have found it to be the one that works best for us.

Communicating Everything

Knowledge is power, so we tell everybody everything. We are a large organization. We have 3,600 employees, of which roughly 225 are investment professionals. Communication by rumor is one of the most corrosive elements in any organization. Even if we are not sure yet how something is going to change, even if we only have ideas about it, we present these ideas tentatively to people whenever possible, saying, "Here are the alternatives that are being examined." A problem with thi approach is that people often get attached to one o the alternatives, but a worse problem is having peo ple wonder about what is going to change.

Facing Mistakes

Changing one's mind is not a mistake, but ther are times when we do make analytical mistakes. W should be able to admit them and say, "I got thi wrong," knowing that others will say, "Thanks fc telling us so quickly." We regularly give hig bonuses or attach a discrete increment to th bonuses of people who, despite the prospect of max imum potential public humiliation, changed the minds about a stock that they recently convince managers to buy. We want to encourage that kind c honest, forthright behavior. This does not mean th we accept being wrong often, but it does mean th we highly value confronting mistakes and takin steps to correct them as soon as possible.

Our most brilliant analysts, our best portfoli thinkers, make mistakes that they are not proud o but understanding where to go next is importan How do we unwind the position, where do we p the money, what did we learn? Is there somethin wrong with the process? Did I get too carried aw by something or other?

In order to counterbalance the focus on mi takes, we have a weekly meeting in which part the time is devoted to reviewing everything that t analysts did right the previous week. For examp we recently had some great success with a sto because our analyst gave us an earnings estima higher than the consensus. She stuck her neck o on this, and we never let that go by unnoticed. V praise it and keep revisiting it. I might mention three weeks in a row. We try to elevate all success

[3] *The General Theory of Employment, Interest, & Money,* Book Four, Chapter 12 (New York: Harcourt, Brace, 1936).

even subtle ones, to a level of visibility that puts the "mistakes" in a larger, more constructive context.

Creating Ownership

In the old days, when we were primarily an industrial economy, the military model of control and command (what Brinson called fear and force) worked, but it does not work today in investment management, in my experience. We try to create a sense of common ownership in the department by having analysts supervise each other, by having analysts train each other, and by getting analysts involved in a wide variety of other things that would normally be thought of as governance. For example, three times a year, the analysts do a self-evaluation of their quantitative and qualitative skills by using a process that they invented. I review these self-evaluations with each analyst and have been impressed by their candor.

In general, analysts are broadly involved in the governance of not only their departments but also of the equity division as a whole. We also get analysts involved in marketing, of which we do a fair amount in the mutual fund business and an increasing amount in the institutional business. Portfolio managers and analysts seem to be spending a lot more time marketing than they used to, but the advantage is that it gives them a sense of ownership.

At any particular time, we also have people working on a variety of special projects. For instance, we currently have a task force that works on how we can improve our work on security valuation. Some people rotate on and off the task force, and some people, who think this is the greatest thing they could be doing because they have a great impact throughout the equity division, remain on it. We have another group that works on earnings surprises to see how we can better understand the significance and the informational content of positive and negative earnings surprises. In addition, we have an analyst running a users' group with the systems department.

Every analyst who wants to manage a person gets a chance to do so. This business has a critical shortage of people who enjoy managing people because the glamour is more frequently attached to managing money. In our department, if an analyst wants to manage a person, that analyst can manage one of our 18 investment associates—people who work with us for a couple of years before going to business school. Managing an investment associate is a good way to get started and find out if you like managing, and your productivity will tend to go up when you get one of these associates to help you, so lots of people like to do it.

Finally, to challenge analysts, we simply let them change industries. For example, our beverage analyst is about to break in another analyst on beverages so he can follow his interest in financial stocks. We are getting to the point where relatively senior people are training other relatively senior people in industries the latter know nothing about but to which their curiosity is pulling them.

Evaluating and Compensating Analysts

The process of developing and challenging professionals leads naturally to appropriate evaluation and compensation.

Evaluation Issues

Three crucial observations apply to evaluating analysts: purely quantitative systems do not work; portfolio managers' opinions are highly variable; and people work all year long.

First, the basic reason quantitative evaluation processes do not work entirely is that measuring an analyst's impact on an organization is complex, difficult, and often has unintended results. For instance, if we tell analysts that they are going to be paid on the basis of a year-end evaluation, and if those analysts have a wonderful first half of the year, we have created an incentive for them to coast for the second half of the year. A worse possibility could occur if an analyst has a horrendous first half. We have then created an unreasonable incentive for the analyst to take inappropriate risks for the next six months. We have created a situation in which the analyst might think: "How could my evaluations be worse? The bonus is gone, so where is the harm in rolling the dice on a particular stock?"

Purely quantitative systems also discourage late-in-the-year work. The really good analysts are frequently ahead of their peers regarding stock insights, and if we tell analysts that we are going to evaluate them on their December 31 results for that year, they may not be as adventurous in the fourth quarter as they were earlier in the year.

Second, portfolio managers' opinions are highly variable, so a system in which the analysts are evaluated entirely by portfolio managers is suspect and does not encourage creative, independent thinking. Although as a fiduciary, an analyst is obligated to take a strong position, but an analyst will be unlikely to take a strong position in a situation in which disagreement, conflict, and so forth are career jeopardizing (and net-worth jeopardizing).

Third, management tends to want to pay for what it thinks analysts have done in the relatively recent period, but people work all year long. Therefore, we do our evaluations three times a year. We try to document everything during the evaluations, and people are paid, in part, for the change in trend in their work. Another reason for the constant evaluation—the three-times-a-year process—is so we can reiterate what we are trying to do as an organization. If we have five goals, maybe three of them will be emphasized throughout the year and two of them will not. The more often we review the goals, the better off we are.

We wrestle with other evaluation issues as well. Rosenberg mentioned the importance of distinguishing between being right and being right for the right reasons. In order to make this distinction, we look at every single action that an analyst has recommended—what we owned before the action, what we owned after the action, how well the stock performed relatively and absolutely, and the impact of purchase and sell recommendations on portfolios. Recommendations that do not result in actions are harder to evaluate but just as important. When analysts recommend an action that is not taken, the missed opportunity may end up costing us money or saving us money. We need to be able to quantify that situation to some extent, and we have actually worked out the following way to measure the results of missed buying opportunities.

We create a phantom portfolio consisting of a certain percentage of the daily trading volume of those stocks for which a strong buy recommendation was made but not implemented; then we compare the profit-and-loss statement of the phantom portfolio with the profit-and-loss statement of the actual portfolios.

We always learn something about the opportunity cost of listening to, or not listening to, an analyst when we analyze unimplemented recommendations. For example, we recently had a lot of pressure for a lot of reasons, internally and externally, to buy a stock at $75 a share. It looked good on certain quantitative screens, and Wall Street was big on it. Our analyst spent a couple of weeks doing nothing but polishing up the five-year model and came back with the recommendation that we not touch it. A short time later, it was worth roughly $35 a share. We need to be able to capture the value of preventive research such as this. The recommendation did not result in a portfolio transaction, but it did prevent a portfolio transaction that would have destroyed value for our clients.

Another element of the evaluation process is the breadth of impact the analyst has had. We want analysts to have a broad impact throughout the organization and not affect merely one segment, such as growth. We also need to know how well they have implemented their business plans, which describe, among other things, where they want to be at midyear in expanding their stock or industry coverage. The quality of the work they have done on the non-U.S. portions of U.S. companies is also important. Finally, for evaluation purposes, we also look at such factors as how well analysts have anticipated surprises and how well they have carried out the collaborative process, not only with other equity analysts in the department but also with the fixed-income analysts.

Compensating Analysts

Putnam Investments is owned by a publicly held company and thus does not have a partnership arrangement. We pay a salary and a bonus based on multiyear results. One of the things that I personally do, and take responsibility for, is to defer a portion of that bonus into a highly structured product called "The Research Fund" that is run by the research department. The analysts have no choice about deferring that portion into the fund, and the money goes in pretax; we have also worked out a way for an additional portion of the bonus to be voluntarily deferred into the fund by the analysts.

The objective of this approach is twofold. First, it allows our analysts, in a nonpartnership environment, to develop ways of building net worth. Second, it keeps us very focused on investment results; few things focus your investment mind as well as having your own money in the product that you are managing.

Conclusion

So, what is the key to managing investment research professionals? No one key exists, but certainly at the heart of the process is recognizing that clarity of thought and conformity of thought are often at odds. Be prepared to encourage the former and discourage the latter. This objective pervades the approach we at Putnam take to recruiting the right people, developing and challenging them, and evaluating and compensating them fairly.

Question and Answer Session

Patrick O'Donnell

Question: If you make a hiring mistake, how long do you try to turn things around before you part company?

O'Donnell: The minute that I know a hiring decision is a mistake, the person knows it. It is unfair to the person, and it is unfair to the person's colleagues for me to be a moral coward on this issue. I hate to have to let someone go, and fortunately, I have rarely had to do it in the past few years. But when taking action is necessary, we take the responsibility, and it happens fast and with great support, encouragement, and candor.

Question: Do analysts provide formal feedback and reviews of portfolio managers as opposed to only having the portfolio managers review the analysts? And if so, what effect does it have on the portfolio managers?

O'Donnell: Yes, we do that kind of review. All of life is relationships, and it is helpful for portfolio managers to know what analysts think about that particular relationship. As for how it affects portfolio managers, I could not directly relate it to compensation, except to say that if an analyst makes a recommendation that is not accepted but the work was all done correctly and the recommendation should have been accepted, it is worth pointing that out. We are not punitive, however. We are looking for what people are doing right, for things to tell them to do more of. That is the primary spirit and purpose of passing evaluative information in both directions between analysts and portfolio managers.

Question: Do you have a specific way of making sure that your compensation practices are competitive?

O'Donnell: Yes, but it is difficult. We try, through the normal reporting services and any other sources we can use, to understand where levels of compensation are in a select number of firms, particularly those firms we especially admire or those with operations similar to ours. I have our research library continually running standard searches on analyst compensation and portfolio manager compensation to find out what I can. Even if I do not think we are at a great risk of losing people to those admired or similar firms, I want to make sure that our people are fairly paid, and I try to spend as much time on that issue as I can.

Question: As director of research, how do you manage all the varied administrative hassles of the job?

O'Donnell: I do not think I can be all things to all people. If brokers want to talk to me, I take that seriously; any day after 5 p.m., they can make an appointment. Since I started this 5 p.m. policy a couple of years ago, there has been a big cutback on demand for my time from brokers. But those who do come tend to be serious and want to talk about something substantive, and the time is set aside for them. I have no easy answer for the other administrative issues; our computer systems are a great help, but most administration is just hard work and attention to details.

Special Report: Job Satisfaction among Investment Professionals

Luke D. Knecht, CFA
Executive Director
Russell Reynolds Associates, Inc.

Richard S. Lannamann, CFA
Managing Director and Global Head, Investment Management Practice
Russell Reynolds Associates, Inc.

Knowing what motivates investment professionals and understanding the satisfaction they get from their jobs are vital pieces of management information. According to a survey of AIMR members, investment professionals generally derive high levels of job satisfaction, but specific levels of satisfaction and the factors that motivate the professionals, either positively or negatively, differ by organizational type and size and by individual tenure and age.

A key aspect of managing investment professionals is understanding what motivates them—is it merely the dollars? Examining job satisfaction provides a window into motivational factors and has long been a staple activity of management theorists and practitioners. More than 25 years ago, for instance, Frederick Herzberg, a noted management psychologist, published a landmark article in the *Harvard Business Review* entitled "One More Time: How Do You Motivate Employees?"[1] This article has been the most frequently requested of all of the thousands that have appeared in the *Review* and has gone through more than one million reprints. The Herzberg study ranks a variety of factors affecting job attitudes and discusses their impact on job satisfaction and dissatisfaction, based on a study of more than 1,600 employees in a range of industries.

Russell Reynolds Associates thought it would be interesting to apply the concepts of the Herzberg study to investment management professionals by asking them about job satisfaction and what motivates them. We commissioned Wirthlin Worldwide, an independent market research firm, to survey a representative sample of AIMR members about various satisfaction factors. From the initial mailing of 3,000 surveys, more than 600 were returned by AIMR members working in a wide range of functional areas at a variety of small and large organizations. This presentation gives an overview of the results from an analysis of 500 usable completed surveys, followed by a discussion of factors influencing job satisfaction and a look at levels of job satisfaction from several perspectives.

[1]*Harvard Business Review* (January/February 1968).

Overview of Results

The overall survey results suggest that most investment management professionals are relatively satisfied in their jobs. Some 46 percent of all survey respondents are "very satisfied" with their current jobs and 35 percent, "somewhat satisfied"; 12 percent and 5 percent are "somewhat dissatisfied" and "very dissatisfied," respectively. The remaining 2 percent did not respond to the question.

Looking at organization types, 90 percent of the respondents who are working in mutual fund companies and investment counseling firms and 88 percent of those in plan sponsors and endowments/foundations report satisfaction with their jobs (either very or somewhat satisfied). Individuals at banks or insurance companies are least likely to be happy in their current positions, with only 76 percent of survey respondents at banks and 74 percent at insurance companies saying they are satisfied with their jobs.

The functional area with the greatest job satisfaction is general management, with 91 percent satisfied. Portfolio managers rank next, with 85 percent satisfied. At the bottom of the list are professionals in marketing, sales and client service, and those fulfilling asset allocation roles—all with a 78 percent satisfaction rate.

Factors Influencing Job Satisfaction

More than three-quarters of the survey respondents cite four factors that most determine an investment management professional's job satisfaction or dissatisfaction—professional achievement, personal or professional growth, the work itself, and taking responsibility. **Table 1** shows that compensation ranks behind these factors at fifth on the list; only 54 percent of those surveyed cite compensation as a major factor in a positive work experience.

Table 1. Major Factors Influencing Job Satisfaction

	Positive Experience	Negative Experience
Professional achievement	86%	34%
Personal or professional growth	79	37
Work itself	78	34
Taking responsibility	77	30
Compensation	54	40
Career advancement	52	35
Recognition	52	30
Relationship with supervisor	40	43
Relationship with peers	40	28
Impact on personal life	35	39
Status	33	25
Sense of security	30	34
Work conditions	23	25
Relationship with subordinates	21	13
Company policy and administration	9	50
Supervision	9	18

Source: Russell Reynolds Associates.

The positive factors are largely internal and personal in nature (e.g., professional achievement); negative feelings, on the other hand, seem to be caused more by external factors. For example, more than 40 percent of those surveyed cite company policy or administration, their relationship with their supervisors, or compensation as factors that play a major role in creating negative feelings about work. Thirty-nine percent cite the negative impact of work on their personal lives.

In a comparison of the original Herzberg survey with the Russell Reynolds Associates survey of AIMR members, professional achievement ranks as the top motivator on both lists of positive factors. On the negative side, company policy and administration and relationships with supervisors seem to be the primary reasons for dissatisfaction in both studies. Investment management professionals, however, appear to place a higher positive value on personal growth and less value on recognition, suggesting that they are more independent than other groups of professionals. (In Herzberg's study of the general population, recognition actually ranked second in importance as a positive factor.) Compensation and career advancement fall fifth and sixth on our survey list, which are higher rankings than in the Herzberg study. Interestingly, these two factors—compensation and career advancement—would also seem to play a greater role in job dissatisfaction among investment professionals than among respondents in Herzberg's sample, which confirms the importance of compensation and career advancement in shaping job attitudes, for better or worse.

Job Satisfaction: Different Perspectives

Although many similarities remain regardless of how we view the data, levels of job satisfaction do differ as we look at the responses from different perspectives. The results of our survey can be examined across four categories of respondents: type of organization, functional area, size of organization, and tenure with organization and age.

Type of Organization

The survey base was composed of professionals at investment counseling firms (30 percent), banks (18 percent), securities broker/dealers (15 percent), insurance companies (10 percent), mutual funds (6 percent), plan sponsors or endowments/foundations (5 percent), and other miscellaneous organizations (15 percent). **Figure 1** shows that professionals at mutual fund companies and investment counseling firms seem most satisfied (90 percent either very satisfied or somewhat satisfied) and those at banks and insurance companies seem least satisfied (24 percent responding dissatisfied and very dissatisfied).

Some interesting differences exist among the positive and negative job satisfaction factors for professionals at each type of organization. Professionals at mutual fund companies, for instance, are

Figure 1. Job Satisfaction by Organization Type

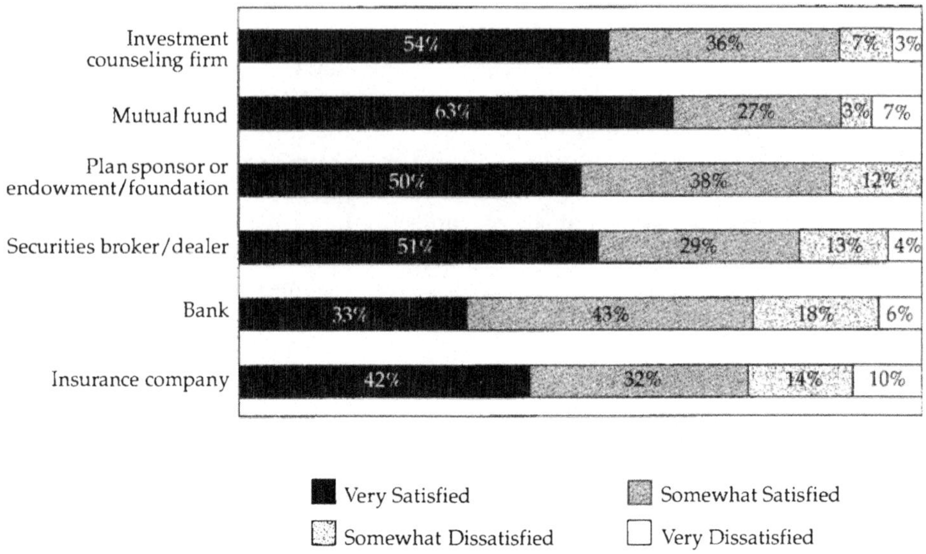

Note: Not all categories total 100 percent because of incomplete response by participants and/or rounding error.
Source: Russell Reynolds Associates.

more likely to cite career advancement, status, and a sense of security as positive factors than are those at other types of organizations. Mutual fund company employees are also the least likely to view any factors as negative, particularly factors such as company/administration, impact on personal life, recognition, and relationships with peers.

Those at investment counseling firms are least likely to cite recognition and relationships with peers and supervisors as positive factors. Compensation, however, tends to be a positive motivating factor for these respondents. At plan sponsor or endowment/foundation organizations, people are more likely to view salary as a negative factor and personal and professional growth as a positive factor.

Those at securities broker/dealers are most likely to view compensation as a positive factor and also most likely to view the impact on their personal lives as a positive factor. At banks, relationships with peers are more likely to be viewed as a positive factor. Work conditions for investment professionals at banks, however, are least likely to be viewed positively. Finally, at insurance companies, compensation is less likely to drive positive work experiences than at any other type of organization. These employees are more likely to cite issues of status and sense of security as negative effects than are individuals at other types of organizations.

Functional Area

The survey respondents included portfolio managers (43 percent), research analysts (21 percent), marketing and client-service professionals (12 percent), general managers (9 percent), asset alloca- tors or "managers of managers" (4 percent), an other professional roles (12 percent). General man agers appear to be most satisfied overall—91 pe cent reported that they are somewhat satisfied c very satisfied with their current jobs, as indicated i **Figure 2**. More than 80 percent of portfolio manag ers and research analysts reported satisfaction wit their jobs; the asset allocators and those in marke ing and client service—more than 20 percent in bot categories—indicated the highest dissatisfaction.

Both differences and similarities exist in the jc satisfaction factors among the various job function Professional achievement and personal or profe sional growth rank highest for those in general ma agement positions. General managers are also mo likely to view company policy and administration positive, probably because they are rating their ov policies and administrations or, at least, are in a be ter position to fix things. On the other hand, they a more likely than other investment management pr fessionals to view relationships with subordinates a negative factor, perhaps because they are the on with the most subordinates to manage. Compens tion and recognition are also less likely to be view as positive factors. For portfolio managers, the re tionship with peers is not as important to a positi work experience as for other investment manag ment professionals. Research analysts are mc likely than other investment management prof sionals to view relationships with their supervis as a positive factor and tend to view a lack of opp tunity for personal/professional growth and car

Figure 2. Job Satisfaction by Functional Area

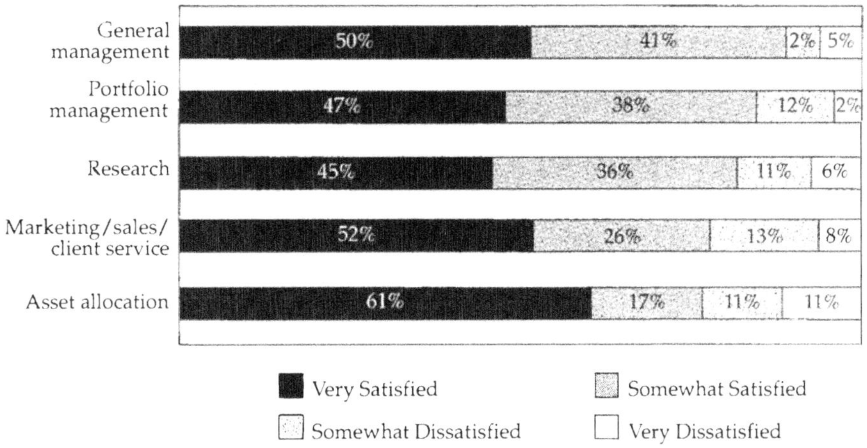

Note: Not all categories total 100 percent because of incomplete responses by participants and/or rounding error.
Source: Russell Reynolds Associates.

advancement as key factors in job dissatisfaction.

For marketing and sales or client-service professionals, the impact of work on personal life is cited more frequently as a positive factor than for other investment management professionals. Somewhat paradoxically, work conditions are least likely to be viewed as positive factors by marketing and client-service professionals. For asset allocators, a category primarily composed of people in endowments, foundations, or plan sponsors, the role of work itself and relationships with subordinates are more likely to be positive factors than for other investment management professionals. Interestingly, this group has the greatest share of both very satisfied and dissatisfied professionals.

Size of Organization

The survey respondents work in organizations with less than $500 million under management (26 percent), $500 million to $4.9 billion (25 percent), $5.0 billion to $49.9 billion (31 percent), and $50 billion or more (14 percent); 4 percent were, for whatever reason, unresponsive to this question.

Figure 3 shows that few major differences in overall job satisfaction exist on the basis of company size. Seventy-nine percent of those at companies with $50 billion or more report they are satisfied; the satisfaction rate is between 80 percent and 85 percent for the other three size categories, and the dissatisfaction rate is lowest for those in the smallest firms.

Size differences do apparently matter, however, in the factors that play a positive role in job satisfaction. The role of interpersonal relationships with peers, supervisors, and subordinates increases as a positive motivating factor with the size of the company. Status and recognition are also more likely to play a positive role in job satisfaction at

Figure 3. Job Satisfaction by Size (Assets under Management) of Organization

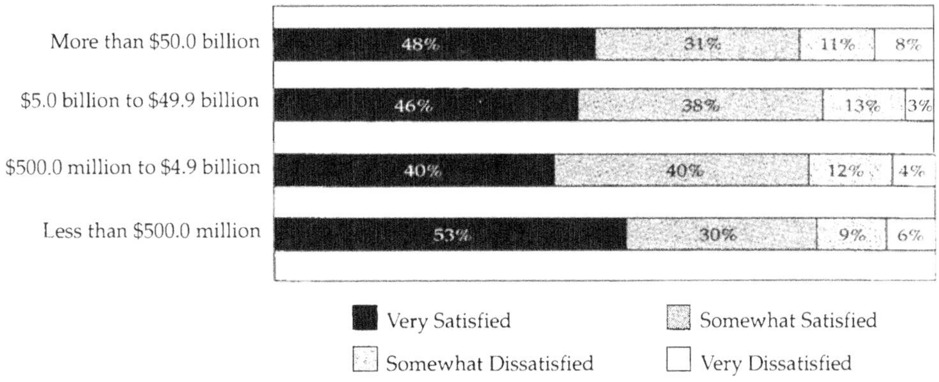

Note: Not all categories total 100 percent because of incomplete responses by participants and/or rounding error.
Source: Russell Reynolds Associates.

Figure 4. Job Satisfaction by Tenure with Organization

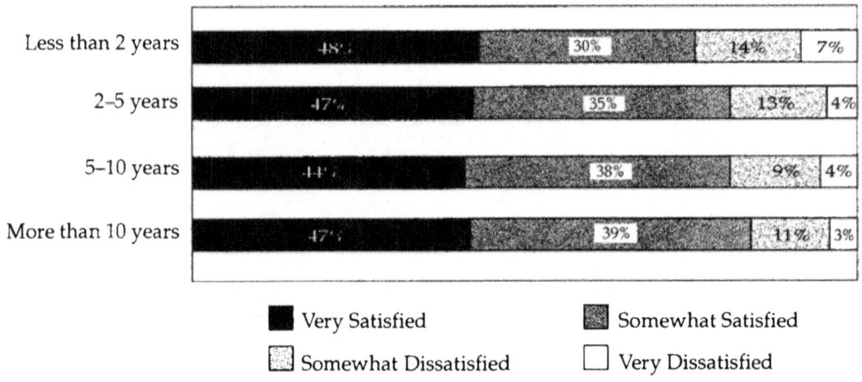

Note: Not all categories total 100 percent because of incomplete responses by participants and/or rounding error.
Source: Russell Reynolds Associates.

large companies. On the other hand, at large companies issues such as personal and professional growth, career advancement, professional achievement, and recognition are more likely to be viewed as negative factors. Also, the smaller the company, the more likely it is that factors such as one's sense of security and responsibility play major roles in creating a negative work environment.

Tenure with Organization and Age

The length of time that investment professionals have been with an organization and their age may also make a difference in views of job satisfaction. The respondents reported tenure with their organization of less than 2 years (24 percent), 2 years to just under 5 years (27 percent), 5 years to just under 10 years (26 percent), 10 years to just under 20 years (18 percent), and 20 years or more (5 percent). **Figure 4** suggests that job satisfaction increases somewhat with tenure, from 78 percent satisfied in the shortest-tenure category (21 percent dissatisfied) to 86 percent satisfied in the longest-tenure category (14 percent dissatisfied).

The biggest differences by organizational tenure among the factors influencing job satisfaction are in three areas: first, the work itself (which is less likely to be viewed as a positive factor by people with less tenure, perhaps because they are responsible for more "grunt work"); second, career advancement; and third, recognition. The importance of recognition to those farther down the tenure ladder indicates the necessity of creating opportunities that allow more responsibility and acknowledgment of achievement as one's caree develops.

Respondent's age categories were less than 3 years (7 percent), 30–39 years (48 percent), 40–4 years (26 percent), 50–59 years (14 percent), and 6 years or older (5 percent). **Figure 5** indicates findings somewhat counter to those for organizational tenure; that is, job satisfaction is higher (86 percent) and dissatisfaction lower (8 percent) fo

Figure 5. Job Satisfaction by Age

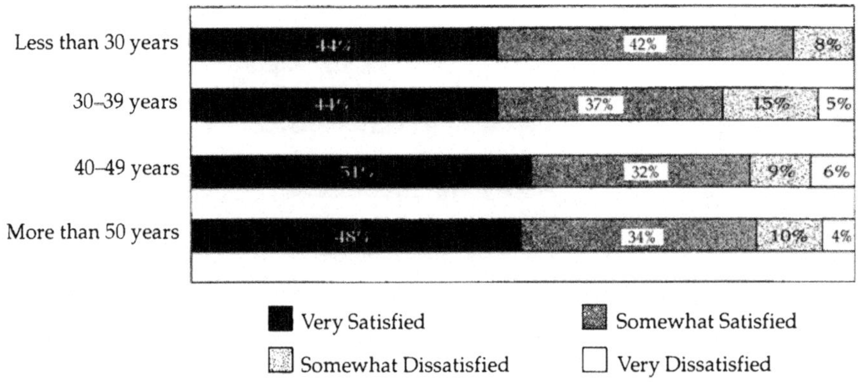

Note: Not all categories total 100 percent because of incomplete responses by participants and/or rounding error.
Source: Russell Reynolds Associates.

those in the youngest category than for those in the oldest category (82 percent and 14 percent, respectively).

Some interesting differences surface in examining the job satisfaction factors by age category. Younger investment professionals focus more positively than their older counterparts on three elements—personal growth opportunities, career advancement, and relationships with their supervisors. The first two elements are understandable for professionals starting out in their careers. The third element indicates that younger investment professionals place value on the mentoring role of more experienced professionals. Older investment management professionals are more attuned than their younger colleagues to the positive impacts of work on their personal lives. Perhaps they have reached a point where they are able to manage their time and their travel in a reasonable way and integrate pleasurable experiences into their work life.

Conclusion

What are the lessons to be drawn from these results? First, perhaps most importantly, the majority of investment managers are happy in their jobs. Although there are some differences according to job function, the size and type of organization, and the age and tenure of the professional, the investment management field clearly provides a stimulating, motivating environment from which professionals derive high levels of job satisfaction. What is surprising is that the factors that affect job satisfaction among investment management professionals are not necessarily what one would expect. Compensation, for example, ranks only fifth on the list of factors that contribute to positive feelings and job satisfaction. Professional achievement, personal and professional growth, the work itself, and related responsibility are more important than money. Investment management seems to be one industry in which the professionals truly love the work.

Building a Global Investment Network

Thomas M. Luddy, CFA
Managing Director and Chief Investment Officer
J.P. Morgan Investment Management, Inc.

Building a global investment management organization that is responsive to client needs is indeed a challenging task. Vitally important in its design is creating, capturing, and communicating an information advantage, with particular emphasis on maximizing the role and impact of the research analyst.

Creating a responsive investment management organization is difficult enough in a rapidly changing domestic context; doing so in a global context is doubly challenging. This presentation provides an overview of J.P. Morgan Investment Management's (JPMIM's) approach to building a global investment network. The history of an investment management organization and the nature of its business have a big impact on how a firm approaches the issue of globalization, so the presentation begins with a brief overview of JPMIM's business operations. The presentation then discusses JPMIM's three-step approach to building a global investment network, with particular emphasis on the role of the research analyst, and ends with some important issues implied in that approach.

Business Operations

JPMIM has $178 billion in assets invested globally and more than 1,500 employees. We have 10 offices worldwide, with an investment infrastructure designed to manage local assets for local clients and at the same time be part of our global investment information network supporting our global products. Our client base is diverse, but we have historically had a heavy institutional component, as shown in **Figure 1**. Our asset mix is evenly divided between equities and fixed income, as shown in **Figure 2**. The key statistics in Figures 1 and 2, however, show that 40 percent of our clients are now in non-U.S. locations, and more than one-third of our assets are invested in non-U.S. securities. Our business is clearly global in nature; therefore, we have tried to create a global investment network that can support local and global client needs—one that knits together research analysts and portfolio managers, central and local offices, and market information and investment products in a seamless fashion.

Building a Global Investment Network

Early in each stage of the evolution of JPMIM's global investment network, we spent a lot of time trying to define clearly the investment process that would underlie our many investment products. By explicitly identifying a process, we have been able to assign clear accountability and responsibility to the many individuals in the network who support our products. Having such a structure of accountability and responsibility is important in enabling us to assess the impact of individuals on our products, to measure individual contributions for compensation purposes, and to identify potential weaknesses in the network that need to be strengthened.

Our overall investment process, each new stage in the continuing evolution of the global network and specific development of our various products—all have been characterized by a common three-step approach: (1) Create an information advantage emphasizing the role of research analysts; (2) use valuation tools to capture that information advantage and (3) communicate the information advantage and the valuation results to portfolio managers in the network so that they can construct disciplined portfolios that meet the many and varied client needs.

Creating an Information Advantage: Research Analysts

The foundation of our processes worldwide rests on the belief that we are able to create an informatio

Figure 1. JPMIM Client Base

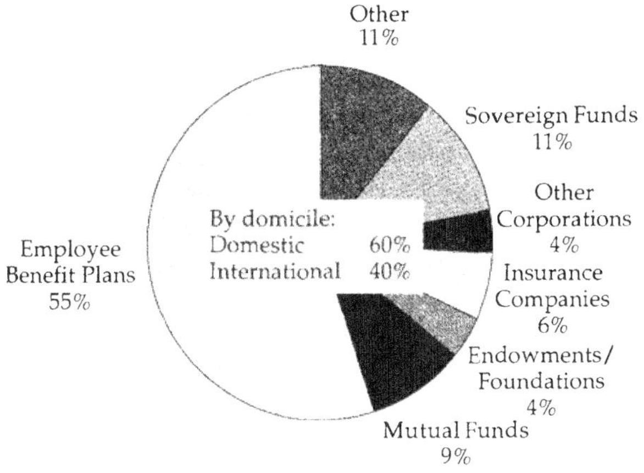

Source: J.P. Morgan Investment Management.

advantage. In acting on that belief, the role of the research analyst is absolutely critical to our success. We have nearly 120 analysts around the world—more than 50 in the United States, nearly 40 in Europe, and almost 30 in Asia. Two particularly important issues must be addressed in affirming the importance of research analysts in creating an information advantage: creating a rewarding environment and choosing a local versus a global focus.

A rewarding environment. Because our process relies so heavily on our analysts, creating an environment that allows an analyst to remain an analyst is crucial. That is, an environment that encourages an analyst to move on for reasons other than personal interest is counterproductive to the best interests of our firm.

Two critical factors that influence whether an analyst remains an analyst are the firm's financial and psychological reward systems. Our analysts can, and do, earn as much compensation as (or more than) portfolio managers, so becoming a portfolio manager does not create a financial advantage. But even more important than the financial rewards are the psychological rewards, particularly the impact and status of being an analyst. We address the issue of impact by insisting that our analysts have an influence equal to that of portfolio managers in shaping the portfolios that are ultimately delivered to our clients.

The issue of status is difficult and requires constant management attention, especially given that external reward systems constantly elevate portfolio managers to a higher status than analysts. The situation in which portfolio managers are given top billing is becoming increasingly true today with the star system developing for mutual fund portfolio managers, and it is doubly true outside the United States because the role of analysts is not as readily accepted in most international markets.

Local versus global. Any firm building a global investment network must decide early on if its research analysts will have a local (e.g., following U.S. auto companies) or global (e.g., following Toyota from a global perspective) focus. At JPMIM, we decided to take the local approach because we believe that the true value added by analysts comes from their doing the hard work—getting to know management, visiting plants, "kicking the tires," so to speak.

As investment management becomes increasingly global, however, local analysts must also gain a global perspective. For example, at JPMIM, we have six copper analysts working worldwide. Although each analyst is responsible for his or her local focus, the six analysts work together so that, as a team, they derive a global supply-and-demand model for the copper industry. This teamwork approach gives each local analyst the global perspective that is critical for a global commodity. These six analysts are then able to take their global supply-and-demand and pricing outlook and apply it locally.

Capturing the Information Advantage: Valuation Tools

The first step of the process is creating the information advantage, but an organization needs to be able to capture that information advantage in a way that drives decision making. Our quantitative analysts create valuation methodologies and tools that allow us to identify the relative attractiveness of asset classes and securities worldwide. For instance, in our equity products, the dividend dis-

Figure 2. Allocation of JPMIM Assets

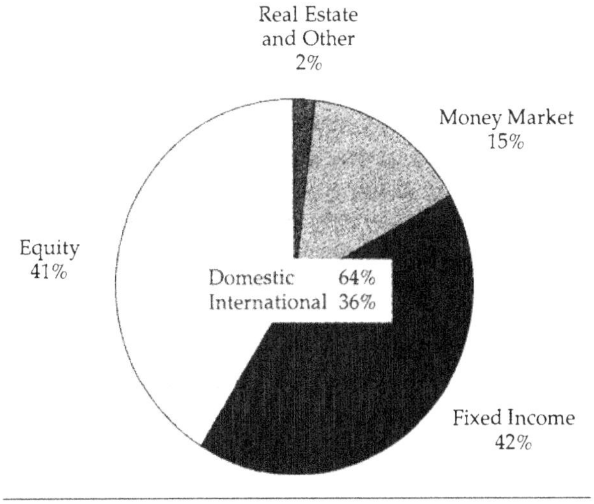

Source: J.P. Morgan Investment Management.

count model is our common language for valuation. Our quantitative analysts also develop valuation models used by our fixed-income and derivatives specialists to value the increasingly sophisticated instruments available in the markets.

Communicating the Information Advantage: Portfolio Construction

In the third step in our approach, the information from the valuation analysis is fed to our portfolio managers to construct disciplined portfolios. To use a fishing analogy, the first two steps of the process (creating and capturing the information advantage) define which areas of the pond have the most fish. In this third step (constructing the portfolio), the experienced portfolio manager fishes in the area of the pond defined in the first two steps to provide the maximum catch from the pond. That is, the portfolio manager uses his or her own insights and experience and combines those with the global analyst network to provide the maximum added value for clients.

The Global Network Approach: Important Issues

The JPMIM approach to building a global investment network is admittedly very specialized and involves consideration of several important issues. First, we want to create an organization with the financial and psychological reward systems that allow individuals to gravitate naturally to their areas of competitive advantage and interest. We do not want someone moving into an area for reasons other than interest or ability. Similarly, career opportunities and the ability to grow and move within an organization are what truly motivate people. Therefore, we want to structure an organization in which if individuals' interests change, the opportunities will exist for them to maximize their contributions.

An important by-product of maximizing individuals' talents is the ability to leverage size and specialization. Being a firm of our size means that our type of global network is feasible financially; if a firm does not leverage specialization, however, it begins to have individuals duplicating roles, and the larger the firm gets, the more difficult the problem of duplication becomes.

Second, we have a collegial environment with a teamwork focus. Each of us depends on others in the organization to deliver the ultimate goal—value added for our clients' portfolios. We need people who are motivated by the success of the team, as opposed to the stardom that they might be able to achieve individually. We also need individuals who can work with other members of the team and get them to do their best in contributing to the overall process. To put it succinctly, we are the antithesis of the star system.

Third, effective communications are particularly critical as a firm develops a global perspective. For instance, although most of our U.S. portfolios are managed in the United States, we also have U.S. portfolios that are managed outside the United States. The performance of both portfolio types should, and in fact must, be similar over time, which requires a focused effort to communicate information on U.S. companies across our network in a timely and accurate fashion. We continually worry about and work to maximize the effectiveness of our organizational communications.

Fourth, a network such as ours is able to fill both local and global product needs. For example, a French fixed-income team in Paris is responsible for delivering French fixed-income products to the local client base, but that team also delivers an information advantage that can be leveraged for our global fixed-income products.

Fifth, as a firm develops a more global perspective, technology becomes a critical success factor. Bringing research analysts, valuation tools, and portfolio managers together to deliver a unified portfolio to the geographical location of the client requires a lot of work on the technology side. Considering everything from multiple time zones to multiple markets, a global network is simply more technologically complicated than a purely domestic one. As a firm becomes more globally oriented, being able to attract and keep good technology experts is as important as being able to attract and keep good analysts.

Sixth, using a global investment network is initially an expensive approach to managing a business, but returns can compensate for that expense. Substantial fixed costs are associated with getting a global infrastructure in place, but as assets are added on top of that infrastructure, the marginal return on incremental assets goes up dramatically. Significant economies of scale arise as a firm gains a global perspective, which has not always been the case with a domestic business. For example, given the importance of fixed income within our organization, we are able to amortize the costs of the equity analysts' research network across a much larger asset base. Our research work is long-term and cash-flow oriented, which ties in nicely with the fixed-income side.

Conclusion

Creating, capturing, and communicating an information advantage—these are the steps in JPMIM's approach to building a global investment network. Our history and evolution certainly make our network unique in many respects, but many of the issues we have confronted would be faced by any organization contemplating a similar process. One lesson we do emphasize is the importance of the analyst's role: The more diverse the analyst's job and the more diverse the impact of the analyst on investment decisions in the organization, the more rewarding the job and the more valuable that person for the organization and the client.

Managing the Virtual Global Organization

David A. Minella
President
LGT Asset Management, Inc.

All investment management organizations face three pervasive challenges: people, culture, and compensation. A virtual global organization, one that transcends national boundaries and markets, encounters and must solve a variety of additional specific challenges—from creating a common vision and goal, to making decisions, to compensating appropriately.

Whether the firm is a global or domestic investment management organization, three things should always be kept in mind: people, culture, and compensation. A global organization, unlike a strictly domestic one, has the added difficulty of having many more moving parts: Not everyone is located in one spot, so not everyone has the same vision, the same goal, and the same compensation plan. After a review of the nature of LGT Asset Management's operations, this presentation identifies the challenges faced by a global investment management firm and poses some general solutions to those challenges.

Virtual Global Firm

Global investment management firms can be divided into two types: domestic dominant and virtual global. The domestic dominant organization is a domestic business with a main office and a centralized decision-making structure that has developed a global business. A domestic dominant is a firm that started out as a single platform for managing domestic assets for domestic clients; over time, global assets were added to the existing structure.

The virtual global organization, in contrast, is not merely a domestic firm with global activities added on. The virtual global organization transcends national and market boundaries; it does not have one central location, but rather, it has a global structure with multiple geographical locations and 24-hour-a-day real-time (hence the label "virtual"), decentralized decision making for portfolios. A virtual global organization has a global distribution of investment staff, research analysts, and business development activities.

Whether viewed in terms of geographical coverage, product or investment mandate, or distribution channel, LGT Asset Management is a virtual global investment management firm. We currently manage $26 billion in global portfolios through eight regional offices with 980 people, of whom 430 are in North America; 350 are in Europe; and 200 are in the Far East. The investment staff of 160 is broken out along roughly the same lines—one-third in North America, one-third in Europe, and one-third in the Far East. LGT manages nine investment products, ranging from global equity, to emerging-market debt, to quantitative investment processes. These products are created in a decentralized fashion and delivered to clients in their various geographical regions around the world. That is, we follow a strictly centralized asset allocation policy, but we are decentralized in our individual stock selections and portfolio construction. LGT's virtual global organization is also characterized by its distribution channels in many markets: About 50 percent of LGT's client base is in North America; 30 percent, in Europe; and 20 percent, in the Far East.

Challenges for the Virtual Global Organization

The challenges facing all investment organizations—domestic dominant or virtual global—always center on people, culture, and compensation. More specific challenges for the virtual global organization include creating a common vision and goal, implementing strategy, making decisions, operating efficiently and economically, and compensating appropriately.

- *Common vision and goal.* All organizations must have a well-articulated vision of what they want to be in the future. The particular challenge for the virtual global firm is instilling that vision in each of the various geographical regions. In addition, regional goals might be in conflict with global goals, so resolving problems could create other challenges. A global organization must somehow continuously meet the needs and desires of local clients while also continuously working toward its global vision.
- *Implementation of strategy.* The challenge to implementing and developing strategy is that a global firm must have both multiple strategies that attack the various markets from a business-development side and a core strategy to cover its investment process. These multiple and core strategies must be consistent throughout the organization.
- *Decision making.* The challenge surrounding decision making for specific portfolio and general business decisions involves whether those decisions are made on a regional (i.e., geographical) basis, a functional basis, or in a centralized environment. In addition, how the choice of decision making affects portfolio and organizational performance ought to be considered. LGT has separated various levels of portfolio decision making; we have a centralized process for asset allocation but regional autonomy for security selection. This multilocation decision process can complicate portfolio construction.
- *Efficiency and economy of operations.* Running a virtual global investment organization is very expensive. If the firm is not careful, efforts quickly become duplicated in various regions. The firm must constantly address the trade-off between the need for overall organizational efficiency and the need for individual regional flexibility. That is, the firm must understand the resource needs of the various regions and be able to fulfill those needs efficiently from its base of operations, but it must also allow the individual regions the flexibility needed to respond to the local markets.
- *Compensation practices.* Compensation is a challenge for any investment organization, and it is particularly so for an organization that is globally diversified in culture, employees, and talent. If a firm were to apply U.S. compensation standards worldwide, it might find itself noncompetitive and unable to attract capable people in some markets or it might substantially overpay in other markets. A firm must take its basic philosophy on compensation, bring it to the various regions, and adapt it to what is acceptable and appropriate in that culture.

Solutions for the Virtual Global Organization

Although different organizations must and will apply specific solutions to the foregoing challenges in light of their own unique needs, all virtual global organizations can consider some general solutions that will help create an environment conducive to success. These solutions cut across geography, language, and culture and include communication, employee development, and management structure.

Communication

Communication is a powerful management tool for any organization and a must for a virtual global organization trying to instill a common vision and goal in multiple locations. For example, in 1987, LGT used faxes to communicate among the various offices. Faxes were the daily newspaper of the company, and everyone in the organization received copies. If someone was having a baby, or someone had a great stock idea, or someone was cutting back portfolio exposure to Japan, it was in the faxes. Today, communication at LGT takes place with e-mail. Some of the personal touch is lost inside a 980-person organization by using e-mail: Everyone does not get every single piece of e-mail that is written. To replace some of the personal touch that is lost with e-mail, newsletters can be used, or people can be rotated among offices.

Furthermore, communication must be two way; one-way communication from the top down is not a form of communication. A firm needs to have bottom-up communication, and inside a global organization, bottom-up communication has to cover many geographical regions.

Employee Accountability, Development, and Compensation

To implement the firm's strategy, the organizational structure must support the goals of the firm and reflect the overall organizational decision-making needs. Distinct, clear accountability and responsibility in every aspect of the business is needed. Without clear mandates and clear areas of responsibility for which a firm can hold people accountable (either by geography or by function), the firm quickly loses control in strategy implementation.

Training and development are also important; the global firm must invest in its employee base. For instance, at LGT we recently started an educational program that brings investment people together, from senior management down through entry-level positions, for 10-week courses (broken into blocks of 2 and 3 weeks) running during a three-year period. We are literally enrolling a portion of the company in a mini-university; a valuable by-product is letting individuals develop bonds across geographical and functional lines that might not have been established without the course. When these people are back in their offices, communications are strengthened substantially inside the organization, not simply among individuals but across departments.

Compensation must be aligned with what the firm is trying to accomplish and must reflect the immutable fact that people are the only assets in this business. We need to understand what our competitors are doing in terms of compensation, both current compensation practices and what appear to be trends in those practices. We must integrate global and local compensation programs that, to the extent possible, align shareholders' interests, clients' interests, and employees' interests.

Management Structure and Decision Making

Added layers of management can accumulate, even when the real intent is to strip those layers out and make the organization less hierarchical. The bottom line is that the organizational structure must support organizational strategy and goals. The very nature of the global organization demands multiple locations, which create cost inefficiencies. Offsetting these inefficiencies are a deeper knowledge of the local marketplace and the leverage to distribute products around the world. Technological advances will also continue to help the global organization "flatten out" the hierarchical structure as electronic communications between our vendors increase and as the quality and cost-effectiveness of video communications improve.

The virtual organization's management structure affects its decision making; the issue circles back to the old debate on regional versus functional authority. All successful global organizations are able to accommodate both sides of the debate: respect for the perspective of the regional experts balanced against the potential effectiveness gained in functional decision making. Distinguishing between two types of decisions can be helpful in assessing the trade-off. Decisions that affect clients directly must be made at a point in the organization as close to clients as possible; this approach mitigates the common, and troubling to clients, view of global organizations as bureaucratic and cumbersome. Decisions concerning the structure and process of the firm, however, should be made at a more centralized point in the organization; such decisions affect clients less directly and require the focus and uniformity typically imparted by a more centralized approach.

Conclusion

All solutions, whether general or specific, to challenges for the virtual global investment organization must cut across geography, language, and culture. Solutions must start and end with strong communication at all levels inside the organization. Solutions must be easily understood and must establish clear lines of accountability and responsibility. Solutions must balance centralized and decentralized decision-making activities, or as LGT terms it, functional and geographical decision-making activities. Global investment management is an interesting business and a constant challenge; solutions with these characteristics will help the global organization meet that challenge.

Question and Answer Session

Thomas M. Luddy, CFA
David A. Minella

Question: In a virtual global investment firm, how do you measure performance?

Minella: We use attribution analysis to measure individual contributions to the portfolios. For example, our portfolio composition structure has five or six people in the organization working on each portfolio. We have segmented their responsibilities by countries or regions. In a global portfolio, we might have U.S., Latin America, Europe, U.K., and Far East portfolio managers, and we monitor their contributions to the overall performance of the portfolio in terms of stock selection and regional country allocation. We compare these managers with an external benchmark and with a competitive peer universe that we develop internally.

Luddy: Because we do not have research set up from a global perspective, we do not have global analysts. We structure our research in terms of local specialists—European specialists and U.S. specialists, for instance—and performance evaluation is in terms of local coverage, seen from two perspectives. First, we use the relevant local benchmarks for the regions of our coverage. We also place a heavy emphasis on stock coverage management; the local analysts control the coverage that they are providing to the network, so how that process is handled is an important part of the evaluation process.

Question: In organizations with local investors, local products, and global products, how do you avoid the risk of trying to do everything in all markets, producing unfocused efforts and unsatisfactory results?

Minella: You have to decide how and where to focus your resources. We are not an organization that has the size to do everything in all markets. Therefore, it is a two-sided answer: We have to pick where we think we can be the most effective as an organization and work where our clients need us to work.

Luddy: Decisions about where to devote resources, which client needs the firm is going to fulfill, which ones do not play to the firm's strength, and which ones would not be in the best interest of the client are constant challenges and part of the continual process of managing. We cultivate resources at the local level when we believe we can create a value-added capability that will be in the best interests of the client and that makes sense from an economic standpoint. We also put resources into an area, even if no business justification exists at the local level, if the information from the area is critical for the global network.

Question: How do you encourage teamwork?

Luddy: Teamwork is a cultural issue; it is an accumulation over a long time of many little things—things that give constant reinforcement to teamwork activities within the organization. And although a firm may have some compensation incentives, if it does not have the constant cultural reinforcement and if it is not attracting people that are motivated by and enjoy being part of a team, annual compensation incentives are not going to foster teamwork.

Minella: If you try to encourage teamwork only with annual compensation incentives, it either will not be effective or will not last.

Question: What is the highest priority for managing a global investment firm?

Luddy: People are clearly the key to managing any investment firm, but as a firm gains a global perspective, the trap that is easy to fall into is for bureaucracy to enter the system. A successful firm may have achieved its success because individuals had responsibility, decision making was decentralized, and the structure of the firm created an environment that retained the best people; in taking on a global approach, that firm must constantly fight becoming more formal and bureaucratic. Otherwise the firm will lose the culture that allowed it to attract and keep the best people.

Minella: People are the raw material in the investment management business. Our greatest challenge is knowing where our next generation of leaders is inside the organization and preparing for the transition of the business to them. One of the important non-people-related issues is technology. Technology will change how we manage portfolios and maybe even how we geographically disperse our resources. Every firm has to understand that technology issues bring another level of both opportunity and complication to a global firm.

Managing Institutional Brokerage Professionals

Stuart M. Robbins
Managing Director
Donaldson, Lufkin & Jenrette

Sell-side investment professionals have an increasingly important role to play in this high-tech age of information overload. Managing these professionals is much more of an art than a science, but several basic principles apply—ranging from recruiting well, to giving full account responsibility, to having fun.

Managing institutional brokerage (i.e., sell-side) professionals is an art, not a science, and we tend to make it harder than it is. Much of the managing task is merely common sense, and the prescriptions should sound familiar, but I am often surprised at how little focus is given to managing sell-side professionals. This presentation will, first, review and affirm the role of sell-side professionals and, second, outline seven simple truths to managing those professionals.

The Role of Sell-Side Investment Professionals

In this high-tech age of information overload, some observers question the nature and relevance of the role of sell-side professionals. Many people in our industry, particularly on the sell side but also on the buy side, believe that institutional salespeople, sales traders, and other people who purvey information to the buy side are dinosaurs. The advent of electronic capabilities and sophisticated information-distributing devices and channels tends to support this idea. I do not share this opinion. Not only do I believe there has never been a better time, or greater need, for the high-quality information produced by Wall Street research; even more importantly, I believe there has never been a more opportune time for high-quality distribution.

Simply stated, those of you who live in the money manager's world have information clutter: You get an 18-inch stack of mail every day; you get 100 phone calls, at a minimum; you receive 30 faxes; and you have multiple screens blaring at you Information is delivered by numerous sources anc strong competitors and at a mind-boggling speed Today, quality distribution is increasingly impor tant to help you get through that clutter, which i where the brokerage professional comes in. Don effectively and efficiently, distribution is the key i the process of bringing the resources of the firm t the client and having a positive impact on a client' portfolio, a notion embodied by Donaldson, Lufki & Jenrette's logo, which reads, "The House Th Research Built."

Seven Simple Truths to Managing

The importance and increasing sophistication generating and distributing information does n change my view that managing sell-side inves ment professionals comes down to seven simp truths: recruit well, give full account responsibilit provide appropriate resources, emphasize clie service, demand performance, highlight corpora culture, and have fun.

Recruiting

First, the most important managerial decisio are made at the recruiting stage. Hiring sell-si professionals is too important to be merely filli slots; never accept less than "top drawer" profe sionals. Looking for those people who are gre marketers is crucial. Hundreds of salespeople a traders in this business are great communicat adept at delivering messages, but few are gr marketers who can bring all the resources of an organization together in a way that affects clients. At DLJ, we look for people who have the ability to add value to the process, who make each contact point better for the client and for the firm, and who have the ability and technique to make a positive impact on client portfolios. Looking for people with these qualities takes time; it is not a short and easy process. The sad truth is that real talent is scarce, and too many firms accept mediocrity rather than holding out for people with the appropriate attitude and mind-set. If you cannot find franchise players who will have an impact immediately on the client base, then you ought to "grow your own." In fact, having a "farm team" is a good strategy. Almost 50 percent of our analysts, salespeople, and traders were home grown; they came to us right out of school for their first jobs. In many cases, these were junior positions, but the people began with real responsibility and most advanced rapidly.

In recruiting these people, the main point to emphasize is not money but organizational values—the career opportunities they can achieve, the resources that will be available to help them, the importance they will have to the firm and to the firm's results, and the culture and family of the firm. These emphases are important in painting a picture of the firm for the candidate and in affirming for the firm that the recruiting process is where managing starts; good managing may well never overcome poor recruiting, but great recruiting can give a real jump start to good managing.

Account Responsibility

Second, the firm must give salespeople and the people who have responsibility for accounts just that—full responsibility and full support. Their job is to develop relations that positively affect client portfolios and to solve problems. Blaming analysts for not making phone calls, traders for inappropriately trading, bankers for blowing the allocation process, or management for not being available is not acceptable. These people must identify the challenges and resolve them. We want them to move aggressively to solve problems when those problems are stomachaches rather than ulcers. We want them to go directly to the key firm personnel, as highly ranked in the firm as necessary, who can help them resolve their problems. Nothing can substitute for intensity of effort and taking responsibility for accounts. Management, in turn, must fully support the people who have account responsibility in their efforts and be willing to devote time and resources to their account needs.

Appropriate Resources

Third, if the firm asks salespeople and others involved with the account to take complete responsibility, it must also give them access to all of the firm's resources; nothing can be held back in supporting these people in an aggressive way. For example, I have flown to Los Angeles for lunch to solve a client problem, and I have phoned from Puerto Rico at 3:30 a.m. to solve another client problem. The best salespeople in the world, the best professionals in the world, need a support network behind them.

Part of providing the appropriate resources is having a good team and knowing that all the parts of the organization are available as needed. Another aspect of providing appropriate resources means allowing what I call controlled freedom, which includes emphasizing appropriate entertainment—pushing for revenue-producing expenses such as client contacts and documentable feedback. Many interesting ways exist to do this kind of work. For example, we have a salesperson who takes different clients jogging every Saturday morning and then buys them breakfast. We have another salesperson who arranges an evening phone-in service to address late-breaking items. Yet another salesperson arranges dinners with analysts and a small group of client "heavy hitters" at which the analysts are given only a minute or two to give their best ideas and each client is then required to dissect those ideas—a kind of reverse feedback.

The bottom line is that, in our business, nothing can substitute for an excellent research product. People who have full responsibility for their accounts and for producing and delivering that product must also be provided with all the support that they need to carry out that responsibility.

Client Service

Fourth, emphasize marketing's three most important themes: client service, client service, and client service. A high-quality relationship is invaluable: It benefits the firm in the obvious economic ways and in the subtler idea exchange that takes place, and it benefits the clients in information delivery, trading services, capital use, and allocations on deals. Sell-side professionals need to thoroughly understand their accounts. They need to delve deeply and broadly into these firms and study the philosophies of the key decision makers. They need to focus on what helps the accounts flourish. As part of this process, the most important thing they can do is listen to clients and communicate their needs back to all parts of the organization: That means research, that means trading, that means the capital markets and syndicate area, and that certainly means management. Remember, our job is to have an impact on client portfolios, not merely to deliver information.

Performance

Fifth, as trite as it sounds, the firm must demand performance. Remember, when we meet the enemy, he is normally us. In the clearest terms possible, the firm must communicate what it wants and expects. In our case, DLJ seeks to be an important resource for all of our accounts, regardless of size. We want to be one of the top three companies in each area of service that we provide. We want to have a multifaceted relationship, top to bottom, between us and our clients' organizations, between the account and the firm. We want to have an improving position by gaining market share; what we actually seek is market share of our clients' minds, not their revenues, because the firm that gets clients' minds will eventually get their revenues. Most importantly, we want to have a clear impact on the account's performance. Asset allocation impact, contributions to the ongoing portfolio process, access to key information providers, and great stock ideas—all are part of affecting the account's performance, but it is the salesperson who must guide the development of this process.

In order for professionals to understand the firm's wants and for the firm to demand performance in the context of those wants, the firm needs to have a very clear feedback and review process. Nothing can substitute for regular reviews, not only for salespeople but for all professionals, and nothing can substitute for strong account profiling. For example, the best profiling I have seen requires taking at least a half-day twice a year with each salesperson and going over all of the accounts. The firm should gather feedback on the salespeople from whomever the salespeople deal with—clients, analysts, traders, capital markets people, whomever.

Any compensation system for salespeople must be fair, understandable, and trustworthy. Unlike most firms in the industry, we prefer a commission system for our distribution personnel because we think it directly relates performance to rewards: We control their account structure and payouts, which we review regularly anyway. One thing that we will not do anywhere in our organization when it comes to compensation is react to competition. We do not meet or even react to outside bids; we simply believe that we cannot tinker with our own internal structure merely to meet the spot market bids that often exist around Wall Street.

Demanding and rewarding performance should emphasize the quality and the tone of the account relationship. How broad and deep are the relationship contacts? How much of the relationship is ongoing regular-way business; how much is new-issue business? The deal allocation process should reflect the fact that the daily listed commissions and over-the-counter sales credit revenue are a much better gauge of relationships than the periodic new-issue order, even though the latter is more profitable. Payouts need to reflect the type of account, the results of the account, and the magnitude of the firm's versus the salesperson's contribution to the results. Payout policy must also be realistic; for instance, one approach our sales manager never takes is to reduce a payout when we are number one in revenues at the account. That payout is a reward for achieving something special.

Finally, accounts that are lost at the client's request should never be replaced: Bad behavior should not be rewarded. But account packages and the account structure for those who are improving in performance should be constantly upgraded. The key focus should be on what constitutes a "good account." A good account is not a question of the cost of servicing the account or of the time required to service it. A good account is a question of having an impact on the account, building relationships, and acquiring revenues and market share.

Corporate Culture

Sixth, the importance of corporate culture cannot be overstated. Low turnover, high performance, and strong profits have everything to do with a feeling of family, teamwork, a shared intensity, and experience. Simply stated, salespeople have to feel that they are an integral part of the firm and an important part of its results; the same goes for traders and other people in the organization. It may sound trite or even silly, but little things do count. Notes and calls on good orders and great accomplishments are worthwhile. Organizational outings that have nothing to do with business are great. Sessions with spouses to make them feel part of the organization ought to be done; even "high fives" between traders at the desk are part of an effective culture. Remember that even the best professionals who make hundreds of thousands of dollars need pats on the back periodically.

The feeling of culture is important, but part of corporate culture must absolutely include the highest standards of professionalism. The employees represent the firm, and anything less than total professionalism, less than total integrity, is simply not acceptable and should not be tolerated. Rules and regulations must be seen in absolute terms, not shades of gray. Even a small thing, such as expense sheets, is not funny business. I am reminded of the story of the salesperson I knew at another firm—thank goodness—who expensed a dinner with a client one night only to find out that the sales manager had dinner with that client the same night.

Having Fun

Finally, having fun is important. Managing by fear is a lousy way to accomplish goals, and the great managers get people to perform beyond their capabilities and work beyond their desires while enjoying every minute of it. This business is tough enough on both sides of the Street without using fear. Of course, in such a competitive business as this, winning and success are important contributors to having fun.

Conclusion

In the final analysis, whether dealing with salespeople or traders, whether buy side or sell side, managing is common sense: goal setting, appropriate feedback, and understanding that investment professionals are creative individuals performing an extraordinarily difficult job in a very volatile environment. My concluding observation is that managing is similar in many ways to being a parent. Most problems in parenting occur when parents choose not to parent: They abdicate the role. Most problems in managing occur when managers choose to abdicate the role. When negative events happen to firms, I am absolutely convinced that supervisory and managerial roles have often been abdicated. The best thing I can say is, if you are going to be a manager, manage.

Question and Answer Session

Stuart M. Robbins

Question: How are you dealing with electronic delivery of research over the Internet?

Robbins: Two points should be made. First, perhaps the most important change taking place that we should all be paying attention to is what is happening electronically. The electronic differences that we will see between now and the millennium will far outstrip anything that happened during the past 10–20 years. In fact, I would argue that in the modern world, the greatest invention that has occurred since the wheel is the communications satellite. Electronic communication is an extraordinarily important issue, and the way we are trying to deal with it is to listen to our clients so that we can be flexible enough to continue servicing them.

Second, I am bothered, to a certain extent, by what has happened to the industry in relation to technology. When I first started in this business, there was a premium for speed, for getting information out earlier than your competitors. Today, everything is instantaneous; all of our electronics, all of our technologies, and all of our polls emphasize speed. If something happens in Borneo, everybody knows about it within 2.5 seconds, so there is absolutely no way for any of us to have a premium for speed.

The result? I am naive enough to hope that what we will get back to is a premium on insight, which is where we were about 25 years ago. In the end, if we can all have our information so automatically, so quickly, what will have a beneficial impact on our portfolios will be the insights we provide that have long-term effects. The most important issue, then, is not how to deal with technology, with electronic delivery of research, but how not to let it overwhelm us to the point of forgetting the basic value-adding device—insight.

Question: Do you think that investment professionals on the sell side get more feedback because of voting and star polls than investment professionals in money management organizations?

Robbins: Feedback is only worth as much as the questions asked. I believe that sell-side people get more public feedback because they have certain polls to deal with and votes that are taken at their organizations; those rankings tend to be important to investment bankers and, to some extent, to clients.

The information those on the sell side can get from clients when they sit and talk to clients, as opposed to merely reading it in a magazine, is terrific. I have never met a client yet who would not tell me anything I wanted to know if I simply asked. Buy-side feedback from us is rarely asked for; in fact, I do not remember the last time a money manager asked me for any feedback on his or her people. If you want feedback, there is no substitute for getting it directly.

Managing Investment Professionals Who Deal with Individual-Client Accounts

Alison A. Winter, CFA
President and CEO
Northern Trust Bank of California, N.A.

Although many management objectives are universal, managing individual-client accounts poses some unique challenges for portfolio managers and firm leaders. Seven components of success can help meet the special challenges of managing investment professionals who deal with individual clients.

Many principles of effective management are fairly constant across account types, but from the portfolio manager's perspective, a number of factors are unique to managing individual-client accounts. From a firm-management perspective, managing those investment professionals who deal with individual clients poses special challenges. Northern Trust Bank of California has $100 billion in assets under management handled by more than 150 portfolio managers operating in roughly 50 locations across the country. Because we deal with individual clients and operate in so many geographical locations, we have chosen an approach to investment decision making that is decentralized in execution but integrated within a broad discipline. In most instances, more universality than uniqueness exists in Northern Trust's approach to managing the individual-client process; it is the nature of the client, not the size of the organization, that is the common denominator of all firms that deal with individual clients. After reviewing some universal management objectives and the unique characteristics of individual accounts, this presentation discusses seven factors for success in managing the managers who deal with individual clients.

Universal Management Objectives

Before considering what is unique about working with individual-client accounts, keep in mind that some investment management objectives (from management's, clients', and portfolio managers' perspectives) are more or less universal. Management basically wants happy clients and successful professionals. Clients want investment results in line with their objectives. They also want regular, personal communication from their portfolio managers in the form of face-to-face meetings and phone calls, not boilerplate letters. Finally, they want to be confident that they are receiving value for the fees they pay. Portfolio managers want financial success, but that is not the only thing they want: They want personal and professional growth. They also want state-of-the-art resources (including technological advances) and to be in an organization that is receptive to new ideas, is vibrant and alive, and is open to change. One of the most important observations I have made is that portfolio managers want to have respect from and pride in the firm with which they are associated. Being good at what we do, respected for how good we are, and valued for how much we contribute are fairly universal objectives.

The Uniqueness of Individual-Client Accounts

Universal objectives notwithstanding, several factors are unique, especially from the portfolio manager's perspective, to managing individual-client accounts. First, individual-client accounts usually involve smaller sums of money than institutional accounts. The size of individual-client accounts typically ranges from $1 million to $5 million in assets. A primary concern of the investment firm is to generate enough total revenues to be able to pay portfolio managers well; thus, smaller account sizes mean heavier account loads for those portfolio managers.

Second, individual client-accounts are often

constrained by client or regulatory demands and implications. When dealing with individual clients, taxes are a very real concern that cannot be ignored and must be factored into investment decisions. Many individual clients put their own constraints on their money managers—such as tolerance for turnover, favorite holdings, and limitations arising from social responsibility concerns. The legal nature of the entities that portfolio managers oversee for individual clients can vary quite broadly and impose unique constraints, for example, a need for a varied asset allocation structure because of the longevity of that particular individual account. A typical family of accounts can include agency accounts that are basically all that individual's own money and, within the same family grouping, IRA rollover accounts, generation-skipping trusts, private foundations, and more—all of which have a different expected life span and thus different asset allocation implications.

Finally, individual clients expect far more personal contact from their portfolio managers than do institutional clients. For that reason, separating investment management from relationship management has proven to be quite difficult, and portfolio managers at Northern Trust combine both roles. The role of relationship management cannot be minimized; individual clients want to have a strong feeling of trust and confidence in the person with whom they deal. They frequently want that person to be a friend, a teacher, and a confidant. The good news relative to this role is that individual clients are extremely loyal. The downside, from a management viewpoint, is that addressing all the issues that provide the level of contact and service that these clients want takes a great deal of noninvestment time. At the same time, the investment management role must take into account that having a single strategy or asset allocation approach for every account, or even every account with common investment objectives and similar investment horizons, is difficult, if not impossible. Meshing the two roles creates the two challenges that are probably most important in our organization: motivating portfolio managers to contact clients frequently and achieving comparable performance across all portfolios. When we add in the complexity of a firm with multiple locations in many different states, meeting these two challenges becomes even more difficult.

Seven Components of Success

In the context of these somewhat daunting challenges, I believe that there are seven components of success in managing portfolio managers in the individual-client investment business. Although each organization has to adapt these components to fit the nature of that organization's business and clients, the components remain the same. These seven components are as follows:

- an effective leader with a clear vision of where the firm is going and what is necessary to get there and with the ability to effectively communicate that vision across the entire organization;
- a clearly articulated investment discipline;
- an appropriate business strategy and the structure to support it;
- the right investment talent;
- appropriate incentives that pay employees well and help retain them;
- a clear understanding of the culture of the organization and how to maintain that culture; and
- the technology necessary to enable the staff to perform their jobs well.

Effective Leadership

The first component of success is effective leadership. The more decentralized an organization, the more it needs strong leadership. In a professional business, strong leaders are needed even more than strong managers for success over time because professionals are intelligent, competitive individuals who do not need to be told how to do their jobs on a day-to-day basis. What they do need is someone who can effectively look to the future, keep the firm competitive, and guide the firm as the markets, the competition, and the landscape continue to change, particularly during difficult times.

An effective leader must first and foremost embody integrity. The investment business has always required that clients trust and have confidence in their portfolio managers; similarly, portfolio managers must trust and have confidence in their leaders. This issue has never been more important than it is today, when too many factors have shaken everyone's confidence and trust. The integrity of the leadership in the organization determines the ethics of the entire firm.

In addition, an effective leader of investment professionals must have strong investment expertise, be approachable and open to new ideas, and be able to welcome criticism. Good leaders must have the ability to manage under constant change. The three V's in the investment business—vehicles, volume, and velocity—will continue to grow at explosive rates. This growth requires effective leadership for deciding how the organization will adapt to these changes. In addition to the three V's, the whole nature of the industry will continue to change, including the competition, the nature of the service and even the nature of the delivery channels. Effective leaders have to be able to manage and adapt the firm to rapid change, and they must themselves have a desire to continue to grow and learn. They should be embracing change in an industry in which opportunity is built on change.

An effective leader must understand that investment management is a creative business and creative people need to be managed accordingly. Not only do people need an environment where creativity can thrive, but creative people also need some order, organization, and discipline surrounding them. One of the biggest needs of creative people is time to be creative. Making time for creativity is perhaps one of the greatest challenges for the managers of portfolio managers who deal with individual clients. Portfolio managers have heavy account loads, and their clients often control their days. At Northern Trust, we try to use technology as much as we can to automate such tasks as letter writing and client presentations. By using templates for client presentations, for example, we can leverage the work that portfolio managers are doing to allow them to spend more time thinking about investments. Effective leaders try to give creative people the time and tools they need to be creative.

Portfolio managers need to be stroked from time to time and poked from time to time. In a year such as 1995, when 70 percent of all money managers underperformed the S&P 500 Index, firm managers have to be sensitive to how individual portfolio managers are feeling about their returns and not simply say, "Work harder" or "Do better." That obviously is not the answer. Portfolio managers are human beings who have lives outside their jobs. When things are not going well in their private lives, those feelings move into their professional lives. The firm manager has to be sensitive to what is going on in an individual's life. Also, portfolio managers, as a group, have big egos, and sometimes those egos need to be managed. After the market took off in 1982, a popular button was handed out by one of the Street firms that said, "I'm not brilliant. It's a bull market." Then, after the correction, another button followed that said, "I'm not stupid. It's a bear market." From the firm manager's perspective, both reminders should be delivered to the portfolio managers from time to time.

Finally, and perhaps most importantly, the leader of an investment organization has to absolutely love the business because it is a business that has to be lived seven days a week; leading an investment organization demands constant thought and attention and cannot be left "at the office." It is not a nine-to-five, five-days-a-week job.

A Clear Investment Discipline

The second component of success is a clearly articulated investment discipline. In an organization as large and as geographically spread out as Northern Trust, discipline can sometimes be compromised, which is almost always a mistake. The first instance in which discipline or a firm's style may be compromised comes in the hiring phase. Most organizations have long, involved hiring processes to make sure the fit between the firm and an employee is a good one. From time to time, firms may be so intent on hiring a certain person that they ignore some lack of fit because they believe that the differences can be worked out, even though some pieces that do not fit with the organization's investment style and overall culture are critical. Too many mistakes of this kind corrupt adherence to a firm's style.

The second way that a firm compromises style is by letting individual managers stray from the discipline, which is certainly a problem when dealing with something as geographically dispersed as Northern Trust's group of portfolio managers. If an organization starts to allow managers to stray from its discipline, straying will soon become the rule rather than the exception, and the result will be confusion and underperformance. In short, the style becomes corrupted.

Two specific aspects of investment discipline are particularly crucial for the individual-client account. First, the sell discipline is a problem because no single right answer exists. When dealing with individual clients, the portfolio manager must consider the after-tax impact on the sell side; short-term decisions cannot be made based on the investment outlook alone. Money paid out for taxes in the short run affects the total after-tax return for individual clients in the long term. Every dollar paid out in taxes is a dollar not invested, and in the investment business, it is money that is in the market that makes the difference.

The second important consideration in investment discipline is the styles that work with individual investors. For instance, a style that relies heavily on market timing is probably not appropriate for individual clients. Examining the S&P 500 during the past 20 years, we find that 90 percent of a full year's return, on average, has been achieved in the single best month of the year. This outcome is even more dramatic with small-capitalization stocks. Investors not in the market during the best month of each of the past 20 years have probably earned a negative return. Therefore, transactions for individuals have to be made on a fundamental basis, in terms of the long-term competitive position of that investment rather than short-term market moves.

For individual portfolio managers, the organization's leaders have to focus on how lasting and fundamental the change will be in the outlook for this investment. At Northern Trust, we look at stock turnover by manager and focus on the two extremes: Too much turnover and portfolio managers impair the long-term, after-tax return; too little turnover and they are not adding value. We work toward a middle ground and try to find the optimal amount of turnover that balances the two concerns, always remembering our focus on after-tax returns.

Strategy and Structure

The third component of management success is strategy and structure. The business strategy is as important as the investment strategy and also must be clearly articulated throughout the firm to all the professionals. Everyone must understand the potential client base and products being offered. Even very large firms cannot deal with every type of client or in every product; no firm can do everything and do it well. An organization identifies the portions of the market and the products to focus on, based on its particular niche, and designates specialists for given segments (large corporate pensions, middle market, or individual clients). To help heighten the focus on a particular market segment, our investment units at Northern Trust are divided into small subgroups. In this structure, taxable individual investors, for instance, are managed by certain portfolio managers and tax-exempt investors, by other managers. We try, to the extent that we can, to group managers by common investment objectives, with growth managers handling accounts in which the objective is growth, and so on. In a small office in a large organization, or in a small firm, accounts can be grouped under a given manager based on the strengths of that manager. The more commonality that exists across accounts, the more consistent the focus on the returns that the firm is trying to achieve.

Whenever possible, we have given managers similar accounts with similar objectives to manage. A portfolio manager who has been successful managing institutional accounts in which the average account size is $25 million or $50 million or $100 million may have no patience at all in handling $1 million accounts in which the clients want to call and ask whether they should sell securities or take a mortgage to buy a second home or a boat. The institutional and individual-client portfolio managers do not think, behave, or act the same way; one is better for one set of clients, and the other is better for the other set of clients. What we are trying to do in our decision structure is to emulate small firms by dividing into small entities sc that all of our portfolio managers have some input into the asset allocation decision process and the stock selection process. The "bottom line" for our kind of organization is that we need a blend o individualism and teamwork. The overall discipline is firmly established by the firm's leaders but the portfolio managers must have a role in the decision-making process because individual clients want to deal with decision makers.

The strategy of the firm must, in turn, be supported by its structure. We try to have as flat an organizational structure as we can within our investment operations. The portfolio managers are closest to the client and closest to the markets. We put them into a structure in which they can meet face-to-face with our clients, which is why we have so man offices. We also try to give them all of the resource they need to stay close to the market. Again, technol ogy helps a lot here: desktop and laptop computer and the information and data services that come i over the wires to those computers. The portfoli managers need to have the tools to keep them clos to the market and close to their clients.

Northern Trust's structure is decentralized, bu we do not take a laissez-faire approach to managin our portfolio managers. Decentralization create risks that must be managed, and we take sever steps to manage these risks. We hire strong profe sionals whose styles of money management are co sistent with our organizational philosophy of mon management. We monitor the performance of all our portfolio managers, and we look at the comp nents of that performance. For instance, we look all trading activity by a manager; we look at ass allocation within our guidelines by policy and obje tive; and we monitor a lot of other subactivities, su as lost accounts, to make certain that, overall, eve portfolio manager is acting responsibly for our org nization and for their clients.

Finally, leaders, particularly in large organiz tions, must protect the portfolio managers from t inevitable bureaucracy that creeps into the wo and the structure; such protection is a job that never finished for the person who is in char Bureaucracy is insidious and has to be weeded c of the portfolio process so that portfolio manag can spend their time managing money, dealing w clients, and doing as little as possible of anythi else that does not enhance the investment process

The Right Talent

The fourth component of success is identifyi the right talent. A leader must know the exact ch acteristics of individuals who are going to fit into organization and meet the firm's strategic objectives, including investment philosophy. Certainly, an individual's investment capabilities are critical. In our organization, we aim for an average experience level of 15 years or more. We get those people in two ways. One way is through hiring portfolio managers from the outside who have the same style of money management as our organization, and the other way is through internally developing portfolio managers from the ranks of individuals in the organization who came right out of college or business school.

We have a blend of the two types of portfolio managers, but we recognize that hiring from outside versus promoting from within is an issue all to itself. On the one hand, management effectively wants no turnover within the firm's professional staff (i.e., having people who stay with an organization for their entire careers). On the other hand, professionals who remain with a firm for 25 years become somewhat insulated from what is happening elsewhere in the market, no matter how much they are out in the market and reading about what is going on. Fresh talent brings in a fresh perspective on things: "Are you still doing this this way?" or, "Gosh, we handled this problem this way where I worked before." Fresh talent coming into an organization prevents the firm from becoming stale and complacent.

Whether hiring from outside or promoting from within, the firm needs a wide range of talents in its portfolio managers. No single person can be an expert on everything; the investment business is far too complex. So, in the process of building and expanding the organization, we must try to bring in diverse talents to add to the richness of our ability to service individual clients. Most of our portfolio managers are managing balanced accounts; even if portfolio managers are skewed toward equities or fixed income, they deal with a balanced portfolio of assets overall. Therefore, we try to bring in people with varied areas of expertise; we believe that diversifying the organization's book of talents provides more leverage in dealing with diverse client objectives and helps achieve success.

As for specific individual traits, the portfolio manager has to love client contact because so much of our business is dealing with individuals. We have to have people who like to deal with their clients, who ultimately have a friendship with their clients, and who do not see contacting clients as a burden. In every client satisfaction survey I have seen over many years and across the different states in which we operate, the degree of client satisfaction is directly proportional to the amount of contact that clients have with their portfolio managers. Client contact is the single most important determinant of client satisfaction.

Our professionals also have to have good business development skills. Many factors are part of Northern Trust's success, and growing our organization is one of them. We look for individuals who are comfortable selling themselves and selling our organization. We have a dedicated business development staff in each of our offices, and we try to protect our managers as much as possible from development calling. But such calls are necessary to close a new relationship; the clients ultimately want to know who they are going to be dealing with and want to see for themselves that these individuals can make decisions, know what they are doing, and are listening to their investment goals. Investors need to have confidence that these people will deliver on those goals.

A successful firm also needs individuals with high intellectual horsepower and with a sense of entrepreneurial ownership of the business. Despite the size of Northern Trust, we want new ideas bubbling up, both investment ideas and business ideas. We want people with some business acumen. They need to understand what drives our costs and our profitability. Re-engineering does not merely apply to manufacturing businesses. Service businesses, including the investment business, cannot be immune from looking at their cost structures and their processes in finding ever better ways to streamline those processes; we use the phrase "better, faster, and cheaper" at Northern Trust. Everything we do should make services better for the client because this business will not be forever immune from pricing pressures. Although the individual side of the business has been relatively immune to pricing pressure in recent years, generally, the changes on the institutional side will ultimately find their way to the individual side.

Incentives

The fifth component of success is total compensation, including incentives. For our firm, total compensation includes base pay, incentive bonuses, and other benefits, such as our 401(k), pension, and employee stock ownership plans; we think the latter three items are valuable in building wealth for our people over time. Twenty percent of Northern Trust is owned by our employees, which makes us probably one of the few, if not the only, publicly traded financial services company that is widely held by its own staff. Despite this ownership and the fact that our stock has done well, our portfolio managers are probably more heavily influenced by cash compensation than by other benefit plans. So, although noncash benefits are important, our focus from a competitive standpoint has been to look at salary surveys to see how we compare with others in terms of base compensation and our incentive plan.

When building an incentive plan, management has to start by looking at what the incentive plan is trying to accomplish. At Northern Trust, we try to reward both notable individual achievements and consistent performance that contributes to group performance. Although individuals might place more importance on their own performance, it is the group performance that the outside world evaluates. We want to promote a proactive interchange of ideas and open-mindedness by encouraging portfolio managers to share successful ideas and talk about what they are doing. We want to promote a "shared destiny" concept among our portfolio managers and increase their ownership in the success of the organization and in our collective performance, not individual performance.

Our ultimate goal in incentive design is to reduce dispersion of returns and increase consistency across accounts and across portfolio managers. We cannot afford much dispersion of returns, especially in a decentralized, multilocation organization. We need to have a high degree of confidence that clients with similar objectives in Chicago or Houston or Naples, Florida, are getting the same, or nearly the same, results as clients in San Diego or Sun City, Arizona. In the old days, when a client was unhappy, management would simply assign another portfolio manager. That approach no longer works. Most likely, clients today would say, "You told me that my account would be managed in your growth equity style. Why would having a different manager matter?" So, we want a fairly tight dispersion around our mean return, and managers must constantly focus on this objective.

Our incentive plans are built around two components: performance (weighted two-thirds) and revenue growth (weighted one-third). Performance evaluation incorporates both individual and group performance, each weighted 50 percent, measured against benchmarks and peer groups. Because our incentive plans are used to support our corporate goals, they are reviewed annually; we rarely make changes in these plans midyear. We involve portfolio managers in discussions of our goals and ask how they think the plans might be changed. Although these plans do not change in the course of a year, they do change over time. In fact, we have made such a change recently. Our equity benchmark has historically been the S&P 500; in order to improve adherence to our overall policy on equity investments (in which we recommend certain percentages in large-capitalization, international, and small- and mid-cap stocks), for 1996 the benchmark will be a blend o three indexes rather than simply the S&P 500.

The second component of our incentive plan is revenue growth. We want to reward two behaviors that augment our revenues. The first behavior tha we want to reward is participating in expanding ou business through new revenue streams and new clients. Second, we want to reward those individual who do a particularly good job of retaining thei book of clients through high client satisfaction Client satisfaction is important to all of us. It is no simply the annual fee that a client pays that is valu able to the firm; it is the annuity stream of fees ove time that is unique in our business. The lower th lost account ratio, the greater the value of that annu ity stream. Thus, we measure lost accounts carefull at both the portfolio manager and organization levels, and examine the reason why the client le and where the funds went, and then we feed tha information back into our incentive structure.

Corporate Culture

Culture and a set of shared values (the sixt factor for success) are absolutely critical and ever bit as important as money management style to firm's success. Culture encompasses everythir from the ethics of the organization to attitud toward the clients, toward the employees, towa excellence, and toward risk. We believe that o culture is unique to us—not necessarily better worse than other firms' cultures but important f our firm to run well. **Figure 1** illustrates four po sible corporate cultures and the requisite leade

Figure 1. Firm Culture

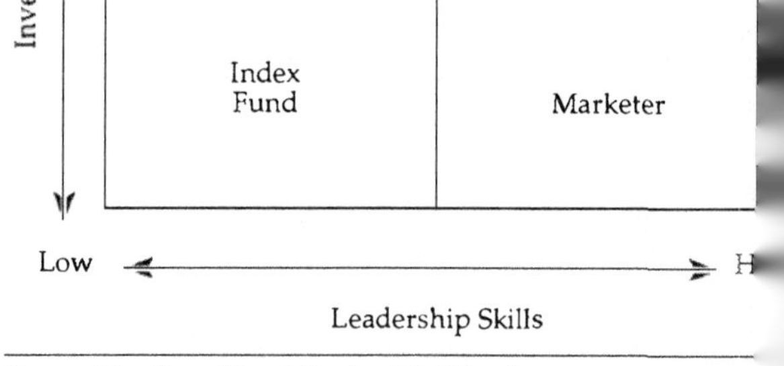

Source: Northern Trust Bank of California.

Figure 2. Stages of Organizational Growth

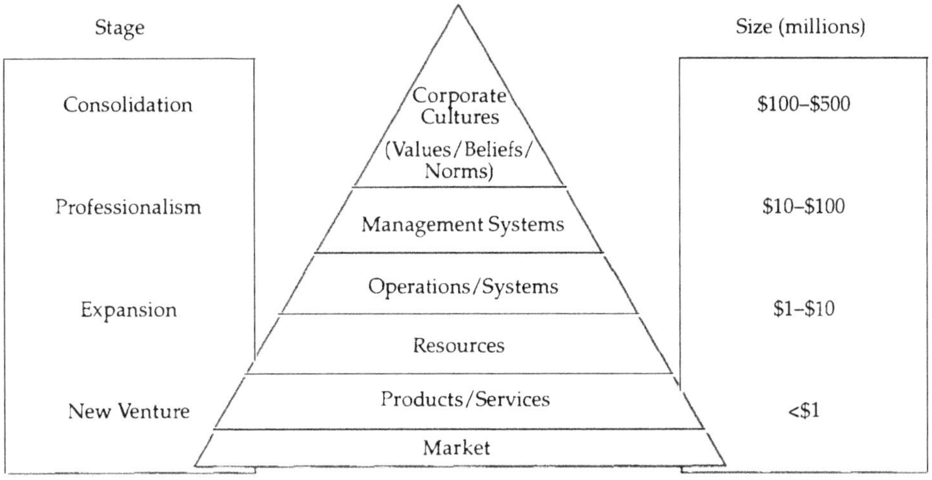

Source: Northern Trust Bank of California, based on data from Eric G. Flamholtz and Yvonne Randle, *Growing Pains: How to Make the Transition from an Entrepreneurship to a Professionally Managed Firm* (San Francisco: Jossey-Bass, 1990).

ship and investment skills for each. The cultures range from an index approach that requires low investment and leadership skills, to star systems and marketing approaches that require only high investment or leadership skills, respectively, to a team environment that requires a complete set of skills. Our goal is to be in the top right-hand corner with a team environment, and to do so, we need somebody leading the organization who has strong investment and leadership skills. The role of the leader is arguably more important in that quadrant than in any of the other three, and the corporate culture is markedly different in that quadrant as well.

Another illustration of the importance of corporate culture, as a function of organizational growth, is shown in **Figure 2**. Each of the components of this pyramid is important in terms of how the firm's management spends time, effort, and thought. A new firm will spend a lot of time on the market and on products and services. Over the years, as the firm grows to be a larger, more mature organization, management, although continuing to spend time on the "pyramid base" issues, will spend much more time on issues such as culture. The important implication is that corporate culture—the firm's values, beliefs, and norms—becomes more, not less, important as the firm matures.

Technology

The final element for success is technology. Keeping up with changes in technology is an absolute necessity in the individual-client investment business, both in how we receive information and in how we communicate information to our clients over time. Technology is changing very rapidly, and it will dramatically affect the delivery channels in our business—from news and research to client presentations and marketing. We involve not only the technical support staff, who are directly responsible for technological changes, but also portfolio managers in the constant re-examination of our systems because they all have to be part of that technological change.

Conclusion

Northern Trust has a structure that is different from other firms' structures; some firms, for instance, have centralized many of the activities and functions that we treat in a decentralized way. The particular structure or the size of the firm is less important than the common characteristics that those of us dealing with individual-client accounts share: the unique needs of those clients and the identifiable components of management success.

Question and Answer Session

Alison A. Winter, CFA

Question: How do you stress their importance to the clerical and administrative people when they can see portfolio managers being managed less, traveling more, and being paid better?

Winter: We try to include our support staff in some of the strategy sessions that we have with our professionals; we also include them in certain training activities, such as tax training, and occasional client meetings. We have more of what I would call "career-track" individuals than "career clerical" people in clerical roles. Most of our portfolio assistants are individuals who have college degrees and probably are going for their M.B.A. degrees at night, which we support. So, they are tracking into a portfolio career. Usually, a time comes when they begin to take on portfolio responsibilities, and then others are behind them to move into their positions. That is not to say we have no career clerical people, but more of our support people are college graduates who know they are going to have the opportunities on the portfolio side if they excel in this area. We also have a bonus system for those who are not included in the incentive plans; for example, when they do a terrific job on a new client presentation or help to save an account where problems needed to be worked out, we can give cash compensation to those people to reward them and make them feel part of the client process.

Question: In the individual-client market, what is the role of marketing? Does the client perceive a difference between business development, relationship management, and portfolio management?

Winter: I distinguish marketing from sales. We do a number of marketing activities to raise our visibility in our geographical markets. Our people, including our portfolio managers, sit on a lot of not-for-profit boards. We sponsor fund-raisers. We hold a variety of functions, with formal speakers and presentations, for our clients to attend. That type of activity is marketing as opposed to selling. We have a dedicated business development staff, and increasingly, those people come from the investment discipline or are individuals who can get up to speed in articulating our strategy and our style—what we like and do not like and our stance on the market today. They have to be knowledgeable—not as much as the portfolio managers, but they have to be able to understand and talk about what we are doing. We expect them to make five to seven calls a day, which we monitor.

I think, for the client, the lines are blurred between marketing, sales, relationship management, and portfolio management. The most successful relationships from our perspective are the ones in which the clients met with their portfolio managers before they decided to hire us and they retained that direct relationship. I think a direct relationship matters more to individuals than it does to institutional clients. On the institutional side, the market has separated relationship management from actual portfolio management. Institutional clients understand that separation. That system may migrate to the individual side. One large organization similar to ours has already separated relationship managers from portfolio managers, but I want to emphasize that I do not think there is one right model.

Question: How many accounts should a portfolio manager ideally cover? How many times a year should a client either talk to or meet with the portfolio manager?

Winter: We look at that situatio in terms of relationships because many family groupings are frequently contained in an individua book of accounts. A seasoned portfolio manager can handle 75 relationships, which can be 130 c more accounts. This account load clearly heavier than that handlec by an institutional portfolio man ager. In terms of client contact, w tier our portfolios. For our large accounts, we want client contact which the portfolio manager is contacting the client, not the clie contacting us, at least monthly ar more frequently if desired by th client. For all other accounts, we want our portfolio managers to contact clients quarterly at a minimum. Some clients do not want much contact; they are bu and simply want their meetings monthly or quarterly. Other clier want to be called frequently, so t amount of contact depends on t individual client.

Question: How do you contr the quality of your products?

Winter: Because we operate i decentralized environment, everything we look at is after t fact, and we recognize that limitation. Trades have already been made. Performance has already been achieved. Therefc we have to rely on our portfoli managers. Having said that, I want to add that we have subgroups of managers across the organization that look at every trade made by every manager. We have a centralized trading operation. If a stock is not on our list, the trading desk will not execute it without making sure that it is a client-directed purchase rather than a portfolio manager deciding, "I like this company, and I will work on getting it on the list later."

We do not have management-by-exception reporting. Our managers actually have to go into our systems and look at the individual accounts for each portfolio manager to see where exceptions to policy exist in terms of asset allocation. We go through peer portfolio manager reviews in all of our offices to see if the asset allocation is within policy, but it is not a science; you are dealing with a variety of individuals. One of the things our managers have to be able to separate out is the "noise" that can exist in our business. If you frequently hear "client considerations" used as an excuse for an exception to policy, you have to look at those cases and see if the client considerations do exist. We are constantly trying to improve our control systems, which is one of the biggest challenges in our decentralized environment and one that we are addressing through new technology.

Question: Do you advocate model portfolios for individual-client accounts, given the unique needs of those accounts?

Winter: We do not use model portfolios. We have looked at that approach from time to time, but it does not work well with the way we are structured. Instead, each of the states that we operate in has its own chief investment officer, and they convene daily (via a conference call) to review the assets on their buy lists. Each state has its own buy list, generated from our guidance list (the broader list of securities that we are following at any given time). The buy list has to meet the screens that reflect our common philosophy. The buy list in Florida is going to overlap with all the other states' buy lists on about 85 percent or 90 percent of the stocks because we are using a common research staff and a common style, growth equity. But there is some individualism in the process at the state level in picking the stocks on their lists; it is not centrally dictated.

One issue that is somewhat controversial right now is that we are currently using BARRA and other diagnostic tools to make sure that in the broad construction of a portfolio, we are not taking unwarranted risks that we will not be compensated for or that do not fit in with the objectives of that portfolio. The reactions to using BARRA have been interesting. Some portfolio managers believe that it takes away their ability to make decisions; others think it is good. I think using BARRA and similar tools can be managed in a way that shows people the benefit of having diagnostics in place. We want to be able to understand not simply what our return is but how we are getting that return and whether we are taking undue risk. Using diagnostic tools need not take away at all from a portfolio manager's ability to make stock selections within the broad list or to participate in the construction of the buy list.

Self-Evaluation Examination

1. Which of the following is *not* one of the equations that Brinson Partners uses to describe its organizational culture?
   a. Philosophy + People + Process = Performance.
   b. Performance = Investment results + Client service.
   c. Performance = Maximum return + Employee satisfaction.
   d. Maximum performance = Maximum business results.

2. According to Brinson, a team approach to investment management is most appropriate when the investment organization has:
   a. Many profit centers and pays people for assets under management.
   b. Many profit centers and pays people for value added.
   c. One profit center and pays people for assets under management.
   d. One profit center and pays people for value added.

3. Which of the following does Fisher use to represent his contention that the successful global organization must have both local knowledge and global vision?
   a. Proximity × Distance = Perspective.
   b. Local knowledge + Global vision = Total presence.
   c. Global return + Local risk = Maximum performance.
   d. Local people × Global systems = Global synergy.

4. Which of the following is *not* cited by Hall as an advantage of constructing portfolios through a team-oriented, majority-vote approach?
   a. Each analyst is a full and responsible member of the portfolio team.
   b. Decision making is not hampered by committees and quorums.
   c. Analysts can prove their abilities and make their case for promotion to portfolio managers.
   d. Client portfolios are nearly identical and dispersion of returns is narrow.

5. The three-step approach to building a globa investment network outlined by Luddy includes all of the following *except*:
   a. Creating an information advantage.
   b. Grooming research analysts to becom star portfolio managers.
   c. Using valuation tools.
   d. Constructing disciplined portfolios.

6. Minella argues that in a virtual globa investment firm, decisions directly affectin the client should be made at:
   a. A centralized point in the firm to gai focus and uniformity.
   b. The point in the firm where resources ar most plentiful to maximize efficiency.
   c. The locations in the firm that house th firm's investment stars to increase clien comfort levels.
   d. A point in the firm as close to clients a possible to minimize client perceptions c bureaucracy.

7. Robbins argues that standards of professiona ism and integrity, as part of corporate cultur must be seen:
   a. Within the overall context of the accou in question.
   b. In absolute terms by everyone in tl organization.
   c. Relative to the individual's cultur background and experience.
   d. Separate from a manager's simple failu to manage.

8. According to Rothenberg, which of t following is *not* an advantage of the multip portfolio management approach?
   a. Relatively small asset proportions a affected when portfolio managers lea the firm.
   b. Manager turnover and rapid accou growth can be addressed by addi experienced managers.
   c. Performance factors can be preserved managers and accounts change.
   d. Clients can readily understand wl proportions of their accounts are m aged by individual managers and wl performance is achieved by those in vidual managers.

9. The capacity to operate within a discipline without being doctrinaire is an example of what O'Donnell calls:
   a. Ethical values.
   b. Flexibility and adaptability.
   c. Ability to handle conflict.
   d. Mental ability.

10. Which of the following observations does O'Donnell *not* apply to evaluating analysts?
    a. Purely quantitative systems do not work.
    b. Portfolio managers' opinions are highly variable.
    c. People work all year long.
    d. Processes for evaluation should discourage both making and publicizing mistakes.

11. According to the job satisfaction survey reported by Knecht and Lannamann, which of the following is *not* one of the four most important job satisfaction factors cited by more than three-fourths of the respondents?
    a. Professional achievement.
    b. Personal or professional growth.
    c. Compensation.
    d. Taking responsibility.

12. Which of the following best describes the nature of positive and negative job satisfaction factors as reported by Knecht and Lannamann?
    a. Positive factors are largely internal in nature and negative factors are largely environmental in nature.
    b. Both positive and negative factors are largely internal in nature.
    c. Both positive and negative factors are largely environmental in nature.
    d. Positive factors are largely environmental in nature and negative factors are largely internal in nature.

13. According to Rosenberg, the question "If you are wrong, what went wrong?" is an example of which of the following fundamentals of managing investment professionals?
    a. Hiring.
    b. Creativity.
    c. Manager stance.
    d. Discipline.

14. Which of the following is *not* one of Winter's seven components for success in managing the managers of individual clients?
    a. Effective leadership.
    b. One or two investment stars to attract clients.
    c. An appropriate business strategy.
    d. A clear understanding of the firm's culture.

15. Dealing effectively with the three V's of the investment business is an example of which of Winter's seven components for successful management?
    a. Investment discipline.
    b. Incentives.
    c. Technology.
    d. Effective leadership.

Self-Evaluation Answers

1. c. Brinson's cultural word equations do not address either level of return or level of employee satisfaction.

2. d. Brinson argues that operating as a team becomes much easier once a firm moves away from multiple profit centers and ceases to use assets under management to determine rewards.

3. a. Fisher discusses the importance of both proximity and distance as vital elements in a global perspective.

4. c. Hall relates that Lincoln Capital Management does not have portfolio managers in the usual sense and that investment professionals are not moved up or down in the organization.

5. b. Luddy discusses the importance of elevating the status of the research analyst, of creating an environment that allows an analyst to remain an analyst without stigma or regret.

6. d. Minella states that different types of decisions should be made at different points in the organization; decisions affecting clients should be made by those people at those points closest to the clients.

7. b. Robbins argues that there are no shades of gray with respect to professionalism and integrity and that many ethical lapses stem from managers abdicating their managerial roles.

8. d. Rothenberg points out that, in Capital's process, clients can know which individual managers handle their accounts but cannot know individual managers' account proportions or performance.

9. c. O'Donnell looks for all four of these traits in prospective research profession als, but the ability to handle the inevita ble conflicts that arise in the investmen business is illustrated by this capacity.

10. d. O'Donnell argues that mistakes are inev itable and effective evaluation shoul encourage and even reward admittin mistakes; the other three observation should indeed be reflected in an effec tive evaluation system.

11. c. Compensation was only the fifth mos important job satisfaction factor as cite by slightly more than half the respor dents.

12. a. Positive factors included such factors a professional achievement and growt negative factors included such factors a company policy and administration an relationship with supervisors.

13. c. Rosenberg contends that an importa aspect of manager stance is learning ho to react to inevitable mistakes and to th people who make those mistakes.

14. b. Winter does not include the presence so-called stars in her list of success fa tors; in fact, she states that her own org nization follows the team environme model rather than the star syste approach.

15. d. Winter makes the point that effecti leaders must have the ability to mana under constant change; a prime examp of change is the explosive growth in t three V's—vehicles, volume, and veloci

Printed in Dunstable, United Kingdom

91222503R00045